Dominic Cook bouldering at Stair Hole Photo: Jonathan Cook

Mike Robertson on *The Swinging Nineties* (FSA) Photo: Jonathan Cook

A trad and a sport climber were once embroiled in a fierce debate as to which was the purest form of climbing. The argument raged on until they sought the advice of a visiting guru from a distant land. The guru, being a clever sort, avoided the question altogether and answered:

'Free soloing is the purest form of climbing. You eliminate the rope, you're up there like a bird or a lizard. It's about as free as you can be.'

Well, that told them.

But, as the guru wandered away, he started to ponder on the wisdom of his words. Something about his answer did not ring true, and it occurred to him that the solo climber was not entirely free, since he must either pre-work the route, to be sure of success, or carry with him the fear of falling to injury or death. If these could be eliminated while some consequence of a fall were maintained, then the climber might truly be free.

Then he thought, 'Well, bollocks to all that philosophizing', and off he went deep water soloing with his mates.

Climbers' Club Guides
Edited by John Willson

Into the Blue

A guide to, and the spirit of, deep water soloing in Dorset

by
Jonathan Cook   (Connor Cove)
Mike Robertson   (History; Dancing Ledge, Durdle Door, Portland)
Steve Taylor   (Durlston Country Park, Stair Hole)
with contributions from
Damian Cook

Maps and Topos by **Jonathan Cook**
Cave Hole Overhead Topos by **Mike Robertson**

 Published by the Climbers' Club

Into the Blue 1996
by Jonathan Cook, Mike Robertson, Steve Taylor

© The Climbers' Club 1996

Cook, Jonathan
Robertson, Mike
Taylor, Steve

Into the Blue

Climbers' Club Guides

British Library Cataloguing in Publication Data

A catalogue record for this book is available from the British Library

796.522

ISBN 0-901-601-59-4

Front Cover: Into the Blue – Damian Cook and the definitive dive from
Rio Point, Connor Cove
Photo: Jon Cook

Rear Cover: Steve Taylor enjoying *Horny L'il Devil* E4 6a
Photo: Mike Robertson

Prepared for printing by the Editor
Printed by BPC Wheatons Ltd, Exeter
Distributed by Cordee, 3a De Montfort Street, Leicester LE1 7HD

Climbers' Club Guides

The Climbers' Club

The publisher of this guidebook is the Climbers' Club, which was founded in 1898 from origins in Snowdonia and is now one of the foremost mountaineering clubs in Great Britain. Its objects are to encourage mountaineering and rock-climbing, and to promote the general interest of mountaineers and the mountain environment.

It is a truly national club with widespread membership, and currently owns huts in Cornwall, Pembrokeshire, Derbyshire, and Snowdonia. Besides managing six huts, the Climbers' Club produces an annual Journal and runs a full programme of climbing meets, dinners, and social events. Club members may also use the huts of other clubs through reciprocal arrangements. The Club publishes climbing guidebooks (currently 15 in number) to cover most of Wales and Southern England. The Club is a founder-member of, and is affiliated to, the British Mountaineering Council; it makes annual contributions to the BMC's Access Fund, as well as to volunteer cliff and mountain rescue organizations.

Membership fluctuates around 900, and at present there are no limits on growth. Members of two years' standing may propose a competent candidate for membership and, provided that adequate support is obtained from other members, the Committee may elect him or her to full membership; there is no probationary period.

Climbing Style

The following policy statement on climbing style was agreed in principle at The Climbers' Club Annual General Meeting on 25th February 1990:

The Climbers' Club supports the tradition of using natural protection and is opposed to actions which are against the best interest of climbers and users of the crags. This applies particularly to irreversible acts which could affect the crags and their environs.

Such acts could include: the placing of bolts on mountain and natural crags; retrospective placing of bolts; chiselling, hammering, or altering the rock appearance or structure; excessive removal of vegetation and interference with trees, flowers, and fauna.

The Climbers' Club policy is that guidebooks are written to reflect the best style matched to the ethos and traditions of British Climbing.

Guidebook Disclaimer

This guide attempts to provide a definitive record of existing deep water solo climbs and is compiled from information from a variety of sources. The inclusion of any route does not imply that it remains in the condition described. Climbs can change unpredictably: rock can deteriorate and the existence and condition of *in-situ* protection can alter. All climbers must rely on their own ability and experience to gauge the difficulty and seriousness of any climb. Climbing is an inherently dangerous activity.

Neither The Climbers' Club nor the authors and editor of this guidebook accept any liability whatsoever for any injury or damage caused to climbers, third parties, or property arising from the use of it. Whilst the content of the guide is believed to be accurate, no responsibility is accepted for any error, omission, or mis-statement. Users must rely on their own judgement and are recommended to insure against injury to person and property and third party risks.

The inclusion in this guidebook of a crag or routes upon it does not mean that any member of the public has a right of access to the crag or the right to climb upon it.

Before climbing on any crag in this guidebook please read any appropriate access and conservation notes.

6

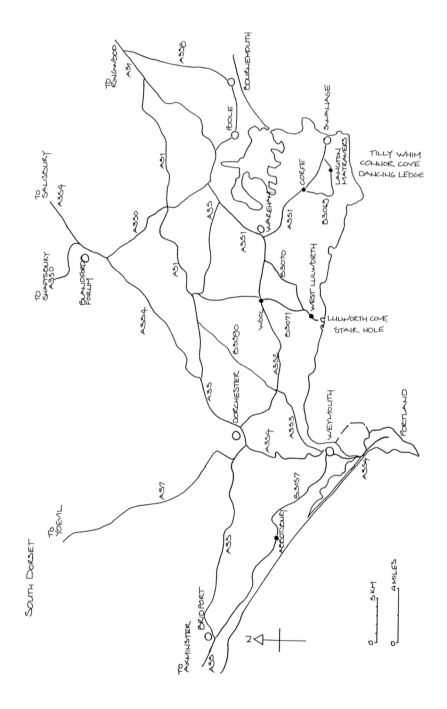

SOUTH DORSET

TILLY WHIM
CONNOR COVE
DANCING LEDGE

LULWORTH COVE,
STAIR HOLE

TO RINGWOOD

A31

A350

BOURNEMOUTH

POOLE

SWANAGE

A31

TO SALISBURY
A354

A350

CORFE

LANGTON MATRAVERS

A35

A351

A351

B3069

WAREHAM

TO SHAFTSBURY
A350

BLANDFORD FORUM

A31

A351

WEST LULWORTH

B3070

A354

B3390

WOOL

B3071

A35

A352

DORCHESTER

WEYMOUTH

PORTLAND

A354

A353

A37

A354

B3157

A354

TO YEOVIL

A35

ABBOTSBURY

BRIDPORT

N

TO AXMINSTER

A35

0   5 KM

0   4 MILES

Contents

Acknowledgements

This guide would never have occurred without the inspiration, guidance, and support of many people.

The spark that set the flame was the front cover of the 1986 *Swanage* guide, with Nick Buckley soloing *The Conger*. For most of us, this route was the first taste of deep water soloing, and what a way to begin. Thanks, Nick.

Jon Biddle, Jon Williams, and Crispin Waddy began the trend of deep water solo first ascents in and around the Swanage area. They showed what could be done, and between them accounted for many diverse solos.

Thanks to Tom Prentice at *Climber* for allowing us to indulge ourselves with articles in his magazine. This demonstrated to us the level of interest out there, and gave us the opportunity to make the phrase 'deep water soloing' known to everyone.

Thanks also to the Climbers' Club, and in particular our editor, John Willson, for going out on a limb and publishing this guide.

David and Teresa Mockford did the typing and formatting for the original Portland manuscripts which made up the interim solo guide. Also, Simon Cook has done an excellent job annotating the topo diagrams.

To our chicks: thanks for washing the salt water out of our clothes and saying that we look 'really ripped' in all of our photos.

A special thank you to those who presented photos for inclusion, including Mark Williams, Helen and Neal Heanes, Pete Oxley, and John Fletcher. Thanks also to Max Hodges for the meticulaous care taken with the processing of the photos for printing.

The final mention goes to our current (Rockies Climbing Shack) and future (Five Ten, Mammut, Boreal, DMM, Prana, Animal, Killer Loop, and Speedo) sponsors. You make it possible for us to climb. Keep sending the gear. Cheers.

JC, MR, ST   May 1996

Editor's Note

As a boy, years before I became aware of the existence of the term 'rock-climbing', I used to love 'bouldering' off Godrevy Point in St Ives Bay. (I read in the latest edition of a magazine that this has *now* become a bouldering venue!) The landings on soft sand or loose pebbles were fine, but it was especially fun when the tide came in and I could just plop into the water (no boots or chalk to bother about getting wet, of course). Much later, traversing the overhanging cave wall to the start of *Moonraker*, I pulled off a handhold and landed in the brine. Not so much fun this time, but still painless (except for the mad dash back to the car for a change and down again to beat the tide).

Then last year, while editing Nigel Coe's definitive *Swanage and Portland* guide (Climbers' Club 1995), I kept coming across this mysterious term 'deep water' and my mind reflected on youthful experiences. However, it was The Cook Brothers' sumptuously illustrated article in the May 1995 *Climber* that truly set the imagination alight, as I am sure it will have done for many.

So when I heard that the authors were looking for a publisher for a guidebook devoted to this activity, I set about persuading the Club that we ought to take it on. This does not signal an abandonment of our primary aim of providing definitive climbing guidebooks to the areas of Wales and Southern England. Rather, this work should be seen partly as a natural adjunct to the 1995 guide, and partly as an experiment in publishing booklets of a specialist nature. And what better subject could we have chosen than this 'adventure climbing' *par excellence*? A W Andrews would surely have approved.

The authors have adopted a more relaxed style than the norm for our definitve guides, which seems wholly appropriate; and we have departed from our 'house-style' in a number of ways to accommodate the content. The traditional Swanage right-to-left order was felt more suited to the natural approaches for the cliffs included as well as to the historical development. However, the order of sections and routes within these areas varies. The locations will always be clear from the topos and descriptions, but care would be needed in relating them to the 1995 guide. Likewise, the deep water soloists seem to have adopted some unofficial nomenclature: in particualar, The Amphitheatre has become known as Lime Kiln Cave.

As well as setting aside a couple of pages at the end for writing in new routes, we have left some white spaces throughout the book where they naturally occur in the hope that you will record your adventures, perhaps even paste in your own photos, to provide an expanding base for future guides in this new genre.

I am very grateful to the authors and their helpers for their speed and efficiency in putting the book together, to Don Sargeant for his help in preparing the artwork for the printers, and to Nigel Coe for bringing to bear his extensive and unrivalled knowledge of the area and his thoroughness in the course of a lightning proof-read.

JW   May 1996

10

Deep Water Soloing Aptitude Questionnaire

Here is a little questionnaire to determine whether you have the makings of an obsessive deep water soloist, a sport climber, a dyed-in-the-wool trad climber, or are perhaps just normal. Try it now, before you read the guide. Then, try some of the routes and answer it again to see if you have moved up the evolutionary scale.

	A	B	C	D

1 Why do you climb?
   a) Because it's there
   b) Because you're nails
   c) Because it's fun
   d) Because it's spring-tide

2. What's the most important thing in climbing?
   a) The mountains
   b) You
   c) Adventure/friends
   d) A calm sea

3. When do you climb?
   a) Weekends
   b) Every day except rest days
   c) When you feel like it
   d) When your boots are dry

4. What makes a three-star route?
   a) The guide book says so
   b) It's one of yours
   c) You wet yourself on sight
   d) You don't have to wait for high tide to fall off

5. What do you wear to the crag?
   a) Ron Hills and Millets fleece
   b) Boreal vest and sponsor's lycra/cotton leggings
   c) Any old cacky shorts
   d) Bugger all pal, it's lovely!

6. You're on a route with loose holds. Do you
   a) Jumar past the loose section?
   b) Hammer them off and up the grade?
   c) Go for it and try not to pull hard on them?
   d) Tap the limpets so they stick on tight?

7. Which do you fear most?
   a) A fatal accident
   b) Tendinitis
   c) A crap summer/work
   d) Aquascrotum

	A	B	C	D

8. What kit is essential?
   a) Helmet/full rack
   b) Gri-gri, double mambas, la Strapella, hypo-allergenic chalk substitute, etc.
   c) Boots and chalkbag
   d) Sponge-on-stick

9. A friend is having trouble on a route. Do you
   a) Call the 'copter?
   b) Sandbag the bastard, he shouldn't be so cocky?
   c) Give beta/assistance as required?
   d) Warm up the camera flash?

10. The route you want to do has a fatal reputation. Do you
    a) Tuck your trousers into your socks?
    b) Top-rope it to death before your high-profile ascent?
    c) Wait for your friend to bolt it up?
    d) Hide out of sight and make spooky noises to scare the shit out of the next party?

11. What's the biggest threat to climbing?
    a) Young hooligans with bolts
    b) Old farts with attitude
    c) Ten pints of lager
    d) Raw sewage

12. It's Winter. The days are short and cold – the rock is out of condition. Do you?
    a) Head to the mountains for some real adventure?
    b) Pump plastic and work on that one finger pull-up?
    c) Put up with crappy conditions and bin the really shitty days?
    d) Join us in Mallorca for fun and frolics?

Mostly...
'A' responses: There's still a chance you may enjoy deep water soloing, but it's harder to swim in a helmet.
'B' responses: You impress the hell out of me – sorry for wasting your time.
'C' responses: Smart move. Deep water soloing is for you. Hope you keep it up - it's a source, change your life – swear to God.
'D' responses: Messiah! Spread the faith.

History

The Beginnings...
When did the madness creep in? Nick Buckley was possibly the first to give in to the urge when he soloed *The Conger* at Connor Cove. He even set a precedent by ensuring a canoeing cameraman was present to record the event. As dedicated deep water soloists have found out since, boats can be mighty useful. Nick also went on to bag an early solo of *Freeborn Man*, his own route, which had already become infamous in 1979 as one of Swanage's first E4s. A man clearly possessed.

A lull followed, broken in 1985 when Pete Oxley soloed the pleasant *Troubled Waters*, to the right of *Freeborn Man*. Around this time, a film crew arrived in Swanage, and, among other things, caught Martin 'Basher' Atkinson in the act of giving *Freeborn Man* its first on-sight solo.

The Enigmatic Approach
1986 brought fresh insanity, mainly in the guise of Crispin Waddy. A man with a mission, Crispin took advantage of some good September weather to produce a fine collection of quality solos at Connor, with the best being the superb *Fathoms*, a brilliant flake-line. Phil Windall also got in on the act, soloing the long-winded *That Disillusioned Feeling When You See Your Jumper Disappearing Beneath the Waves*. Phew!

1987 stayed quiet, but was followed by a vintage year: 1988 saw much activity, with the action no longer confined to Connor Cove. Stair Hole at Lulworth Cove and the Tilly Whim sea-ledges were added to the solo venue list. At Tilly Whim, an inspired Jon Williams kicked off the year with his first ascent solo of the utterly atmospheric *Camel Filter*, a deep water soloist's dream come true. He returned when the sea had warmed a little and added *Slap Ya Dromedary*, and also *The Hump*, in the same area.

Lulworth Cove
Over at Stair Hole, the diminutive but exceptionally strong Jon Biddle created the powerful *Anarchy Stampede*, a boulder-problem route which still invariably resists the static approach, and Jon Williams traversed through the west side of The West Cave to give birth to *The Maypole*. Back at Connor, Waddy soloed *Moving Away from Rufty Tufty*, whilst Biddle added the enjoyable *The Musharagi Tree*.

1989 started in March, when Waddy returned to capture the *Furious Pig*, a bottomless route requiring an innovative access approach. This year also saw Portland's first solo, with Oxley's *This Is the Life* (he was right), a superb groove with a shallow landing. The remainder of the year was quiet, apart from a visiting Andy Donson's solos of *Sardine Liberation Front* at Durdle Door, a thoroughly photogenic line on one of the coast's most beautiful features, and his *Turkish Delight* down at Tilly Whim.

New Blood Arrives

Into the 90s, with many gob-smacking lines to fall at every venue, and entirely new solo venues to be discovered. Summer 1990 saw an on-form Biddle solo (wobble) his way up the right-hand finish of *The Conger* to produce *Jellied*. In August 1990 a new team emerged in the form of the Cook Brothers. An enthusiastic assault on the beautiful streaked wall/flake-line at Connor West saw a happy Joff Cook top out, with *...And Captain Blood's Cavern* being the prize. Dominic Cook returned in September to conquer the slightly scary direct finish to *The Conger* – with epics ensuing before success – prompting the title *Snap Crackle and Plop*.

1991 was strictly a Stair Hole affair. Of note were Biddle's excellent *Herbert the Turbot*, a wicked and committing problem across to the hanging slab in the southern side of the western cave (the scene of many a splashdown), Joff Cook's *Captain Bastard Got There First*, a short groove he obviously beat someone to, Biddle's superb *Truth, Justice and the Ragamuffin Way*, a somewhat longer groove-line, and Damian Cook's ultra low *Does Leviathan Plop Float?* in The East Cave.

A Quiet Summer

Was the summer of 1992 that bad? A quiet year, with inactivity broken only by Oxley's low-level *Sliding Down the Banister*, and his solo of his excellent bolt line *Horny L'il Devil*.

The Counter-Trend Begins

1993 broke the spell and a new contender appeared. Mike Robertson was a man clearly in the Biddle/Cook mould regarding unencumbered climbing. One of his first offerings was *Spittle 'n' Spume*, a pleasant traverse down on Portland's east coast in an area called Cave Hole, a cliff that would later reveal vast untapped potential. He also added *Intimate Dancing* to his tally, whilst another newcomer, Steve Taylor, crimped up the groove of *Robertson's Jam*.

The Mark of the Beast

Amazingly, Cave Hole fell quiet again, while an active Oxley felt the urge at Stair Hole, with a return to solo two of his bolted lines there. His 1987 traditional line of *Mark of the Beast*, now freshly retroed, became *the* solo test-piece, whilst the high and slappy *Stagedivin'* became *the* sought-after on-sight.

Robertson, Mark Higgs, and Gideon Fitch joined Oxley for the memorable group on-sight of *The Laws Traverse* (perhaps the most popular solo at Stair Hole), with Robertson returning later to claim *The Walkin' Dude*, a line that really could have done with a decent tide. In the meantime, Damian Cook was active at Connor Cove, filling in some memorable and scary gaps. June was his month, with *Tsunami* and *Leap of Faith*, two bold numbers with big-fall potential.

Exploration Begins in Earnest

1994 was a another memorable year, with many locals forsaking ropes to join in what had become a cult following. It was a year of consolidation at Connor Cove and Stair Hole, with the new-routing confined to Portland. The bolted area of Lime Kiln Cave/Beeston came under scrutiny, with the lines of *Etna*, *Bay of Rainbows*, and *The Bellybutton Traverse* falling to the soloing shoes of Taylor, Damian Cook, and Robertson respectively. On the on-sight front, Robertson and a bouldery Mark Williams traversed out of the pebble-beach area of Cave Hole to give an amusing *Memory Lane*, and Robertson found his niche when he grabbed *Foxy Chicks* and *The Big Easy*, both in yet another undeveloped sector.

The summer also saw some established and committing bolt routes soloed, both on Portland and at Stair Hole. At the recently developed White Hole North, a sunny August day saw Robertson achieve solo success on his own powerful and slappy *Dead in Europe*, whilst Taylor appeared on the same day and balanced his way up *The Skin Trade*, two audacious solos in an atmospheric area indeed. Down at Lulworth, a bicep-stricken Joff Cook cruised *Animal Magnetism* for the camera, and many other lines saw numerous (and group) solos from all local head-cases.

The Long, Hot Summer of 1995
To say 1995 eclipsed all previous years would be something of an understatement. The statistics speak for themselves: a total of thirty-eight deep water solo new routes, plus a large handful of established routes being freshly soloed and thus added to the soloist's definitive tick-list. The grade of the routes attacked on sight rose dramatically, with the die-hards shrugging off repeated splashdowns and simply donning fresh boots and chalkbags for another go.

The deep water soloing mentality had truly arrived, and the weather probably helped a little.

First off the blocks was Damian Cook in mid-April with *Ixtlan*, a fine flowstone groove in The Big Easy Sector. The finest April weather in history dried out all those important little places, leaving May conditions as good as they get. Cave Hole was definitely *the* venue, and furious on-sight new-routing ensued.

What, No Roofs?
An on-form Robertson blasted across the roof of one of the finest caves to produce the classic 25-foot roof-climb of *Crab Party*, and bagged the strangely hollow arête of *Up the Grotto*. Damian Cook discovered another superb cave, and hung around for a while to create the fantastic *Octopus Weed*. Meanwhile, Robertson got up early for a good tide and attacked the rather blank continuation to *Spittle 'n' Spume*, a line he considered virtually impossible two years earlier, and emerged with his *Bare Reputation* intact (just). Over on the west coast, an exploratory Damian Cook discovered the delightful Jacuzzi Boulder, a steep, technical slab with some superb short lines on perfect rock, and a deep rock-pool beneath.

Preaching to the Masses
New-routing aside, May was also memorable for the Cooks' excellent Deep Water Solo article in *Climber*. Some superb colour photos armed newcomers with the

necessary information and inspiration. *The Conger* had never seen so many solo ascents.

Into June, with some friendly competition fast developing, and not much time for consideration... The first line in the huge cave by the single crane fell to Robertson with his ascent of *Desperado*, and Damian Cook returned to collect the audacious overhanging arête line of *Lick of the Cat*. Robertson fully breached the *Ixtlan* face and found it to be *Russian Roulette*, whilst Damian cracked the plyometric *Reel 'Em In* on *The Big Easy* face. The nerve-racking bulge of *Karma* fell to Robertson, whilst Damian Cook claimed the cranky *Flipper Force* on the left side of the Grotto Arête.

A fast and furious summer continued, with Joff Cook emerging from work commitments in the far South-West to produce his own test-piece to ponder – *Tentacle Master*, a powerful line that sees few on-sights. Steve Taylor (eventually) topped out triumphantly in August with *Aquamarina*, and a smitten Robertson finally nailed *The Swinging Nineties*, a superb and very inverted roof-line in the waterfall cave, and Portland's hardest deep water solo to date.

Elsewhere, Stair Hole saw a full-on revival, with some amazing efforts from inspired individuals. Joff Cook, fresh from his success on Cave Hole's *Killer Loop*, adopted Stair Hole as his new home, and made the first solo ascent of *The Gates of Greyskull*, with a snapping-at-the-heels Robertson following 1½ hours later. An in-love Damian Cook made it a threesome a fortnight later. *Stagedivin'* saw its first on-sight solo from John Fletcher, whilst Robertson finally hung in on his direct start project to *The Laws Traverse*. The interior of The West Cave saw some new additions from Joff Cook and Robertson, the hardest being *El Guapo*, a ferocious test-piece from Joff Cook which would merit a full F7b, with the ascent being a very wet eventual on-sight.

The Interim Guide

Mid August also saw the printing of the interim guide, *Portland's Deep Water Solos,* by Robertson, a useful booklet which was quite out of date within a few weeks of its appearance.

Into September – the season finally drew to a reluctant close when Robertson suddenly realized the full implications of the boulder-strewn water in Dancing Ledge's West Cave zawn. Four solos of established routes soon followed, the hardest being *The Pump Will Tear Us Apart*, a fine and tremendous offering requiring full Lulworth bicep strength.

A final mention for 95 goes to an ever adventurous (Colorado resident) Andy Donson, who appeared briefly at Connor Cove and snatched the first on-sight solo of *Swordfish Trombones*, all those years after Waddy's bold attempt. A fine effort.

To the future. Where will it end? There's more out there, although much of it is desperate. Take a look at the project section and help yourself to a slice of the action. May the hot summers continue!

Deep Water Soloing

Tides

The tidal phenomenon is the periodic motion of the waters of the sea due to changing combinations of the gravitiational forces of various celestial bodies, principally the moon and the sun, upon different parts of the rotating earth. The tides can be either a help or a hindrance to the deep water solo climber. Generally it is an advantage to have plenty of deep water underneath you, though particularly high tides may mean access to certain routes becomes more difficult (such as *Crab Party* on Portland and *The Laws Traverse* at Stair Hole).

When the sun, earth, and moon are aligned (new moon and full moon), the gravitational effects of sun and moon act in the same direction, causing the maximum resultant force upon the oceans that results in the highest possible tide for that area. The low tide at such times will be the lowest possible tide. Such tides are referred to as spring-tides and occur once per month. When the moon is in its first and third quarters (i.e., the sun and moon are at right-angles to the earth), the resultant force is lower, causing a much lower tidal range. Such tides are referred to as neap-tides. They also occur once a month and are equidistant from the spring-tides.

On Portland, where the tides have perhaps the greatest impact of all the areas, the difference between a high spring-tide and a high neap-tide can be as much as 1.3 metres, or 4 feet. This variation can be a major factor in the character of a route.

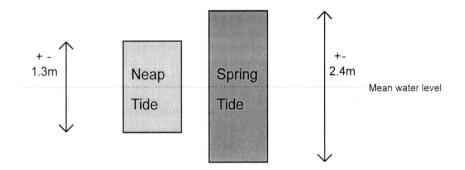

Certain routes may be viable only on high spring-tides, e.g. *This Is the Life*. On a normal low tide, there is only a rock platform under this route, so don't try it then. On a high spring-tide, there will be up to 6 feet of water underneath, making it a far more viable proposition (unless, like many, you prefer at least 20 feet).

Mike Robertson using the chalking stick on *Skeleton Surfers*
Photo: Jonathan Cook

Mike Robertson leaving the bench seat for *Esmerelda's Monkey*
Photo: Helen Heanes

Jon Biddle ... on Freeborn Man. Photo: Pete Oxley

Pete Welch ... off Freeborn Man. Photo: John Fletcher

Group Outing on *Troubled Waters* Photo: Steve Taylor

'Only the best route of all'
Simon Cook on *The Conger* Photo: Jonathan Cook

Along the Dorset coast, there are two high tides and two low tides per day (known as a semi-diurnal tide). With each cycle, the times of these tides move on about 45 minutes, with successive high and low tides being separated by about six hours. This is useful knowledge if you have witnessed the tides for one day and need to predict tide times in the near future.

However, the most reliable method of predicting tides is to use a tide table, available at most newsagents in the area, as well as Easton Post Office on Portland. (Rockies Climbing Shack in Fortuneswell also displays local tide times on a notice board). These are published annually for the Portland and Swanage area in a small booklet. Not only do they give you the high and low tide times, but they also tell you the height (above mean sea-level) of the tides, something you need to know for those marginal routes which need a spring-tide. A spring-tide is between 2.1 and 2.6 metres. A neap-tide is 1.2 to 1.5 metres. The tide tables cost only about 50p and are very simple to interpret. The importance of the state of the tide is noted in the route descriptions. Remember, however, that these tables are based upon Greenwich Mean Time (GMT), so add on one hour to the times during Summertime.

Grading System

The intention of the dual grading system used in this guide is simplicity. It will show you, along with route descriptions, roughly how hard, safe, scary, sustained, high, or slappy a route is, for its grade.

The 'S' Grade

S0 Safe at most tides, not particularly high crux moves. Avoid bottling out of an S0 or an S1 if possible. These are essentially fairly safe. Climb until you fall. Commitment normally pays off!

S1 Care required; either tide/depth needs checking, or maybe there is a high crux.

S2 A little more care than S1. Probably spring-tide only (higher water levels) – check tide timetables – spring-tides occur roughly every two weeks. 'Landings' more important – maybe a crash landing into shallow water required, or possibly a jump-off route only (rather than a fall-off one!). Likely to have a high crux. Take care.

S3 A connoisseur's route – water present for psychological purposes only; you can't really afford to fall off an S3! Imminent failure on the route would require a full body length crash landing into deepest water available. It almost goes without saying, wait for a full spring-tide for these!

To summarise, S0 is safe as houses and S3 can be death on a stick!

'E' or 'XS'

A considerable amount of soul-searching went into the overall grades contained in this guide. The difficulty was in defining the solo grade - whether to use English,

French, or XS grades. Most readers will be familiar with the first two – the XS grade was reintroduced to grade 'ungradeable' routes such as those on chalk cliffs or weird cave climbs, when it directly replaced the 'E' grade, yet still utilized the technical grades as before. It became incorporated into the deep water soloing scene in the South in the 80s, and seems to be here to stay.

Essentially, all grades in this guide are precisely what the first ascensionist gave them. Please forgive us for any confusion. In brief, an XS 5c could be E1, E2 or E3. The route description and the visual impression of the line in question generally offer many clues. XS grades occur predominantly in the Cave Hole routes. The remainder of guide is more specific in its English/English-French grades. Have fun, don't take them too seriously folks – after all, it's only water.

Tactics

Now why do we need a section on tactics? Surely you just get on the route and go for it, don't you? Well, not necessarily, and a lot of the time there are ways and means to make the routes more accessible, easier to read, and psychologically more comfortable.

Footwear and Chalkbags
Starting with the obvious. If you're out to take on anything near your limit (i.e., you might fall in), then multiple pairs of climbing footwear are going to be useful, preferably old pairs. The best are climbing slippers, for two reasons: they're easy to swim in and they dry out more quickly. You'll spot those who have already been in, as they'll have black or green feet from the dye in the leather. If you've more than one chalkbag, that could be useful also. Carry only the minimum of chalk required for the route, as blocks which get wet aren't any use once they have dried out. It's been tried. Boots and chalkbags dry out especially quickly when tied to a roof rack or hung out of the car window when driving between venues.

There are a number of cunning alternatives to carrying a regular chalkbag (usually by those with only one). These include rubbing chalk into cotton shorts, carrying chalk in pockets, or even making disposable bags out of plastic bread bags, wire coat-hangers, and cotton, or tin foil held on with masking tape. One recent idea was to sew extra side-pockets on your shorts, baggy enough to hold chalk.

The Bench Seat
The bench seat [photo p.16a] was an excellent innovation by Mike Robertson. It can be used to access comfortably routes with a hanging start such as *The Great Shark Hunt* (Connor Cove) and the White Hole routes. Clipped onto an abseil rope and lowered to level with the start of the route, you can abseil down to it, drop onto the seat and remove your harness while sussing out the moves in a pump-free position. The alternative on such routes of trying to unclip from your harness on just an ab-rope is a real drag, and you'll most likely be pumped before you start.

Knotted hemp rope is another useful alternative and you can Tarzan your way in quickly and hit the route with minimal fuss. A seasonal knotted hemp rope is bolted in place giving access to the routes in the Grotto Arête sector on Portland, lending a swash-buckling aspect to this sector.

Swim Approach

Certain routes such as *Tsunami* and *Surface Tension* have a ledge at the bottom which you can swim to and dry out on before starting the route. If you want to do this, one useful technique is to tie your boots onto your head with your chalkbag string, with the bag on top, ease your way into the water, and swim keeping your head up. It really works.

The Chalking Stick

The chalking stick [photo p.16a] is most useful for the short deep water soloing/bouldering in caves such as Stair Hole West Cave or the *Octopus Weed* cave. It was devised to get chalk onto holds which can be dampish on routes which are so steep you don't want to stop moving and chalk them before cranking them. It's made by attaching a piece of sponge to an extendible pole (e.g. a broom handle). It's smart to tie a loop onto it so that you can carry it on your back whilst getting into the routes. Basically, dab damp or hard-to-see holds.

Spotters

Another point to mention about these caves is that certain routes require a spotter. This doesn't mean that someone gets to tread water waiting for their friend to fall on them, but low, bouldery routes may have a ledge or slab between the climber and the water under a short section of the route. The role of the spotter is to push a falling climber away from such dangers into the safety of the Big Blue. Examples of such routes are *Contortions*, *Showtime*, *Stagedivin'*, and *Killer Loop*.

Wetsuits

Well, it's a bit of a wuss-out but if you're the sort of person who feels the cold, wear 'em if you've got 'em. 3mm shorties are the best as you'll have more mobility. Also, if you're going to get any flexage in the photos you had better make it armless. Well, these things have to be considered.

Pre-working the Solo

Obviously, nothing is more pure than an on-sight attempt soloing a route with no boots, chalk, or clothes, and with a blindfold on, but some of the most aesthetic routes are likely to be right at your limit and no one is going to begrudge people pre-working routes at the limit of their ability so as to prepare for the solo. The by-word here is fun, not ethics.

Now there are a lot of solos which you just cannot work effectively, such as those on the Portland roofs. But the steep Stair Hole routes and some on Portland are bolted, allowing a pre-work, and many of the Connor Cove routes can be top-roped or shunted.

The bottom line is that if you think you could get it and the water looks OK-ish, then why not go for the on-sight solo? It's exciting for you and highly entertaining for your mates. Once you've taken that first splashdown, you'll never look back.

Hold Marking

One other dodgy technique involves marking holds on blind or slappy moves. This is usually done by chalking holds near the tops of routes when you just don't want to come off after completing everything up to there (e.g. *Aquamarina*).

An extreme version of this was used to bag the first solo ascents of *The Gates of Greyskull* at Stair Hole, where the final move involves dynoing for a blind narrow slot. The perpetrators used a marker pen to draw cross-hairs indicating where the slot was (well, it is 40 feet up, and we'd fallen a few times already). Don't worry, after a winter's rain the marks wash off.

Splashdowns

It may seem a little negative to be discussing this, but what if disaster is beckoning? You have reached a crux and cannot work it out, you have just snapped off a hold (obviously quite unlikely), or you are just plain pumped out. If you have any intentions of attempting any of the routes described in this guide, you need some pointers on 'splashdowns'.

If you are at Conner Cove (or on some routes at Stair Hole), safe splashdowns rely on excellent penetration (no comments, please!) as cruxes are fairly high and fortunately the water is very deep – around 30 feet. Try to assume the shape of a vertical torpedo to ensure a clean entry. Awkward landings here have had some interesting results, including a sea-water enema. Do your best to plan your safe descent into the briny.

Portland cruxes are rarely higher than 25 feet from the surface, and as the water depth is not so generous, developing an 'armchair' or 'bunched' landing is advised. An 'armchair' is as it sounds – sit back slightly as you enter (you'll even have your slippers on!). Or the original 'dive-bomb' – not as effective, but take your pick. It may be worth choosing your landing-spot between submerged boulders, remembering to aim for it if you do fall.

Health Warning

Two points to bear in mind. First, diving or jumping into shallow water is a prime cause of spinal injury. Second, the flood tide flows to the east, the ebb to the west, and at certain times these currents are too strong to swim against. One near casualty of Portland's east coast currents was Marie Stopes, pioneer of birth control. You can take precautions by keeping close to the cliff face.

Conclusion

We each have our own sense of ethics about climbing. Therefore make your mind up for yourself which tactics you want to use, whatever makes it fun.

New-Routing and Ethics

This section represents a collection of ideas, rather than a rigid set of rules. Climbers invariably climb as they please – you too can please yourself with regard to the routes contained in this book. Guidelines are useful, however, and they show the manner in which the local activists have developed the area.

First, mention of Cave Hole, in the red hot summer of 1995. The weather prompted an explosion of new-routing, all carried out with the on-sight ethic in mind. Let me explain this. It depicts a ground-up ascent, or attempt, with no recourse to cleaning, route inspection or, especially, prior working of moves on the route.

To ascend a new route in this way is surely the purest form of climbing possible. In the event of a fall, or more correctly a splashdown, the new-router may decide to dry off and try again. He's missed out on the on-sight flash of his chosen line, but he's still on-sighting, because all moves above and including the one he fell off remain a mystery – and therefore still on-sight.

Make sense? Allow me to draw a parallel with Gogarth. The ethic at that most infamous of bold sea cliffs works in much the same way – try telling a ground-up new-router at Gogarth that he's no longer on-sighting, when he's just taken a 50-foot whipper on an *RP2*, and he's resting for another go. Bold indeed. Deep water solo merchants invariably suffer no worse than the dreaded 'cold and wet' treatment, so aside from drying off, a continued assault is inevitable.

Connor Cove has a mixture of traditionally-ascended routes and solos, with all traditional routes since soloed. Some routes put up in solo fashion were totally on-sighted, and some were precleaned, occasionally with great necessity.

Stair Hole has much diversity. It has a mixture of short solos and long traverses, along with two fully bolted cave areas. Many of the bolted lines have been soloed with varying styles. An on-sight solo flash would represent the best style, followed by repeated on-sight splashdowns and eventual success. Next in line is the working of the moves on a rope followed by a solo redpoint, with a roped redpoint followed by a confident solo coming last. But never be sad; a solo is a solo. It feels very different when you're up there. Here are a few multi-ethical examples from 1995:

> *The Gates of Greyskull* F7b+   solo redpoint, third attempt
> *Aquamarina* XS 6b   fifth on-sight attempt, a wet one
> *The Swinging Nineties* F7b   solo after successful redpoint
> *Stagedivin'* F7a+   on-sight solo flash

So, get the message? On-sight is best. I'll save the last mention for White Hole and Dancing Ledge West Cave – two crags where atmosphere confounds the mind and bares the soul. Don't miss out on a route in these areas - you'll never walk the same again.

In this guide, where a first ascensionist is given, that is the first solo ascensionist. A number of subcategories are used. In the First Solo Ascent list, at the back of the guide, the style of the first solo ascent is defined by a number. This number correlates to the following list:

1. On-Sight Solo Flash (New Route)

On-sight solos could have been preceded by a number of splashdowns; thus it is important to state where the first ascensionist has made a special effort (or been very lucky). The route had never been led before, so the first ascensionist had very little prior knowledge of it, including grade, looseness, etc.

2. On-Sight Solo Flash (Existing Route)

Knowledge of the grade of the route before an on-sight solo was attempted is important prior knowledge. Also, any loose rock should have been removed by now.

3. On-Sight Solo with Splashdowns

Just as pure as a flash really, but there has been no pre-inspection and the ascent has still been made ground-up (or sea-up).

4. Solo Redpoint

This is where the first solo ascent of a route was made by a person who had previously roped it (with falls), and therefore had prior knowledge of the moves, although success may not be assured.

5. Post Redpoint Solo

The first solo ascent was made by a person who has already made a successful roped ascent of the route.

6. NYS

If a route has not been soloed (but may have been led on a rope, or top-roped) it will be indicated with a NYS – 'Not Yet Soloed'. These may be the ones to aim for if you want to be famous. They all have water underneath, more or less.

Durlston Country Park

This area is where climbing really began at Swanage. The terrifyingly high and loose cliffs of the Boulder Ruckle await young climbers in search of their first real epics. It may come as a surprise to the reader that this area could contain anything of interest to the deep water solo merchant. Surprisingly enough there are some excellent little traverses, short safe problems, and eerie cave encounters to be had.

Approach
All approaches are described from Durlston Country Park. Durlston Country Park lies just to the south of Swanage, which nestles south of Poole Harbour (between Bournemouth and Weymouth). The Park is well signposted from Swanage town centre. Park your car in the large car-park (about £1 a day) and head for the cliff-top footpath. The Lighthouse sits above The Black Zawn, in between Tilly Whim West and Subluminal. Walk-ins to these two areas should be no more than 10-15 minutes.

Aspect
The majority of routes in this section are on south-facing cliffs. Generally, they will be in the sun until mid evening. As many routes are low-level traverses they require fairly calm conditions. The routes which enter caves/chimneys can often seem damp in any weather, though this only adds to the experience.

Note that all routes at Tilly Whim West are subject to agreed bird restrictions from March 1st to July 31st.

Tilly Whim West

This area lies at the base of the valley running down the eastern side of the lighthouse, centred around the obvious, small box-shaped zawn. Some routes are totally safe, others require a decent tide.

Camel Filter   XS 5c   **S1**   35 feet
A strange and eerie trip through a cave that you would not even know about unless you could climb 5c.
Climb down the corner at the right-hand side of the back of the zawn. This crack soon widens to become the cave entrance, which is a bit tricky to enter. Chimney across the cave, heading for the light at the back of the cave, which is a blowhole leading back onto the ledge. While inside the cave it is possible to fall onto boulders.
FSA Jon Williams (28.4.88)

Llama Roundabout   XS 5c   **S1**   40 feet
A variation on the previous route, taking it into the bowels of the cave.
Before exiting the blowhole, traverse the right wall of the cave northwards and drop down onto an isolated boulder. Traverse the far wall, heading back for the

blowhole to finish. Very weird.
FSA Mike Robertson (14.8.94)

The Hump   XS 6a   **S1**   15 feet
At low tide, the water is only a few feet deep underneath this difficult problem.
Climb down the crack at the right-hand side of the zawn for a couple of feet.
Traverse left along the break to the centre of the back wall and make a series of
long stretches to reach the top.
FSA Jon Williams (6.88)

Slap Ya Dromedary   XS 5b   **S1**   25 feet
Traverse left along the break-line on the back wall of the zawn. Once across the
wall, enter the cave with difficulty (karate kick required) and chimney to the back.
Finish up the cleft; precisely where you choose will be dictated by belly size.
FSA Jon Williams (8.88)

Numb Bum   XS 6a   **S1**   40 feet
The continuation to *Slap Ya Dromedary*, with a finish above not very deep water.
Instead of entering the cave, traverse the left wall of the zawn, around the arête,
and then finish up the very overhanging wall in the seaward face, right of the
obvious flake/crack.
FSA Jon Williams (6.88)

Turkish Delight   XS 5c   **S1**   45 feet
As for *Numb Bum*, but traverse a few feet further left and climb the steep crack to
finish.
FSA Andy Donson (24.8.89)

Subluminal

This is where there may be some crowds to watch your exploits. Be warned, people
with helmets and beards may 'tut' disapprovingly. Take no notice, they are only
jealous.

Much bouldering is possible on the short walls and arêtes beneath the 'main' cliff.
The best outing here, however, is the following. **Note that this route is subject to
an agreed bird restriction between March 1st and July 31st.**

The Subnutcracker Traverse   HS 4b   **S0**   60 feet
An excellent sea-level traverse, possible only in calm seas.
Climb down the groove beneath the start of *Greasy Chimney*, at the extreme
western end of the ledge. Start traversing left, around an arête onto a vertical wall
a couple of feet above the sea. This wall has some perfect positive holds along it.
Keep going until you reach some large boulders at the base of the cliff. Reverse
the route to get back to your gear.
FSA Unknown

Boulder Ruckle

Only one route described here, but it is an excellent sea-level traverse. Similar to *The Subnutcracker Traverse*, but far longer and slightly higher above the sea. From the lighthouse, follow the cliff-top path westwards for about half a mile. This will bring you to a wall running perpendicularly across the path to the cliff edge. Follow this wall, on the lighthouse side, down to the cliff edge. You will find some abseil stakes to take you down the overhanging line of *Ocean Boulevard*, and the start of:

Paradise Street   Hard Severe 4b   **S0**   200 feet
Fine climbing, linking the hard man's *Lean Machine* face with the bumblies' paradise of Cattle Troughs. Worth the effort of the abseil approach, or could be included as part of a sea-level traverse of the Swanage cliffs.
The route-finding is basically quite simple. Follow the break-line leftwards for ages across some steepish sections from the start of *Gaston*. Eventually, you will arrive in a popular climbing area, where there are likely to be plenty of people wearing helmets and beards, who will probably… It is best to solo nonchalantly past them, bidding them good-day and praising their gear-placing skills. Pick a sensible point to scramble up to the cliff-top path to finish.
FSA Unknown

The Cattle Troughs Area

There are a number of possibilities worth investigation here, including *The Beastly Step*, *Blindman's Buff*, *Unknown Ledge Traverse*, *Benny* (pitch 1), *The Eastern Traverse*, and *Clever Dick*. FSA of the last was Andy Donson (28.8.89); probably some or all of the others have also been soloed.

The Swanage Traverse

This is a very long traverse/swim/boulder-hop, starting at Tilly Whim West, and heading westwards as far as you like. The whole thing, all the way to St Aldhelm's Head, is about five miles, though there are numerous exit (and alternative start) points on the way, such as Subliminal, Cattle Troughs, Fisherman's Ledge, Dancing Ledge, Hedbury, Seacombe, Winspit, and Slippery Ledge. Where you decide to finish depends on how fit/keen you are.

It goes without saying, that it should be attempted only on a warm summer's day, with calm seas, and by competent people. Do it with a group as it will be more fun and gives a safety margin in case of difficulty. If you really want to enjoy the climbing, wear an old pair of climbing boots, but don't bother with a chalkbag.

This route is known as **The Cormorant**, and is described in more detail in the definitive *Swanage* guide, page 244. Please refer also to the guide for details of the **bird restrictions** which affect sections of the traverse.

Connor Cove

Connor Cove is the original forcing-ground for deep water soloing and the associated aquatic entertainments, and has probably the most imposing atmosphere of the venues.

Soloing here dates back to the late 1980s, with Crispin Waddy, Jon Biddle, and Jon Williams pioneering the way. Archaeological remnants including Greek pottery and Neolithic arrowheads found in pockets on *The Conger* prove earlier visitors also showed an interest in deep water soloing.

The majority of the routes top out at over 50 feet and although most have their cruxes lower than this, there is certainly potential for some major air-time when falling off. With the exception of only one or two routes, none of the solos here is genuinely risky, but because of the cove's general aspect they all feel and look 'out-there'. This means that there are some excellent photo opportunities, which you can later display on your mantelpiece with pride. 'What's that?' your Northern climbing friends will ask. 'Oh, that's me soloing *Swordfish Trombones*, I think it's E5,' you can reply.

Most of the soloing is focused around The Conger Cave, but other classics, such as *Fathoms* and *…And Captain Bloods Cavern*, are outlying. *The Conger* itself is simply *the* deep water solo. An inspirational route which has hooked many locals into soloing above the sea.

Approach
The walk-in to Connor Cove is just over one nautical mile. Park at Durlston Country Park and follow the private road down towards the lighthouse. You will pass two pylons, which mark the eastern boundary of a marked nautical mile. Follow the cliff-top westwards for one (ordinary) mile to the western pylons. Thirty yards beyond the lower pylon, a track descends leftwards towards the cliff edge. Follow this down to the point where the cliff-top makes a squarish corner and becomes rock pavement. You are now standing over The Conger Cave. This walk-in should take approximately 20 minutes.

Aspect
Summer gradually clears the seepage lines on *The Conger* and *…And Captain Blood's Cavern,* and by April/May a warm day with a low swell brings this venue into shape. From then on, the sea warms through to late September.

Being directly south-facing, it is in sun all day across the cove – except for the *Freeborn Man* wall, which gets it by lunchtime.

Everything is as tall as any sane-ish man would care to solo above the sea, at around 50 to 60 feet. None of the cruxes are above 50 feet and the top-outs are generally very clean.

Large swells change the aspect considerably, and although it is easy to exit the sea in *The Conger* area in choppy conditions, the Funky Wall routes should be avoided if the waves are breaking up the cliff. The most important exits are below *Helix* and at the right (east) end of the Funky Ledge. Check the swell carefully before starting. If the sea is breaking over these, or there is more than a few feet of swell, beware!

Should you be caught out by rain, then you're probably a bit hardcore being there in the first place, but shelter can be found under the roofs just east of the start of *Helix*.

The Conger Cave

The Conger Cave routes are accessed by down-climbing *Helix*, the route coming down the right-hand side of the *Freeborn Man* wall. Otherwise, abseil down this line or from stakes 50 yards east onto the large platform of Fisherman's Ledge and walk around the corner to *The Conger*. Either way, you end up at the base of *Helix* on the ledge/arête at sea-level.

Helix   Difficult   **S2**   50 feet
The corner line and easy way in/out of the cove. Not a true deep water solo for at least the first 20 feet as the underlying ledge juts out. But it does beat setting up an abseil. There are stakes above if a top-rope is needed for getting beginners/jellies in and out.
Climb the corner to a ledge at 30 feet (good diving ledge); then follow the slab/corner on the left past a rusting horizontal stake to finish.
FSA Unknown

Troubled Waters   Hard Very Severe 5a   **S0**   50 feet
[Photo p.16c] Sound jug-hauling above totally safe deep water. An excellent and straightforward introduction before you hit the toughies.
From the start of *Helix*, pull leftwards for 5 feet and then up straight onto the wall. Climb directly up the slab and steep wall to the finish at the right-hand end of the strip roof of *Freeborn Man*. There is the chance of a flagpole pose at three-quarter height.
FSA Pete Oxley (15.7.85)

Freeborn Man   E4 6a   **S1**   50 feet
[Photos p.16b] A benchmark route of legendary quality. Soloing *Freeborn Man* is like leaving school, passing your driving test, or burning down your first public building.
The thin ledge leading to *The Conger* has a small break in it half-way to the first sentry-box. Crimp some fingeries here and haul onto the wall above. Move up and left for about 15 feet to the apex of two flakes. Follow excellent, beautifully formed finger-pockets up rightwards to underneath the strip roof (crux). Move up and left again to two pockets on the lip of the overhang and rock over. S1 for the

28

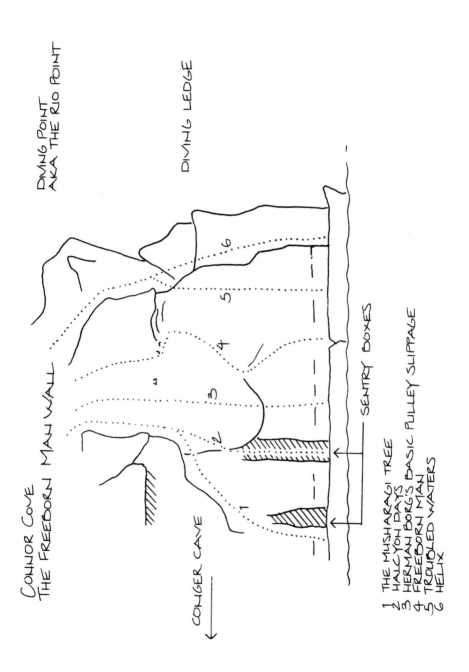

CONNOR COVE
THE FREEBORN MAN WALL

DIVING POINT
AKA THE RIO POINT

DIVING LEDGE

CONGER CAVE

SENTRY BOXES

1 THE MUSHARAGI TREE
2 HALCYON DAYS
3 HERMAN BORG'S BASIC PULLEY SLIPPAGE
4 FREEBORN MAN
5 TROUBLED WATERS
6 HELIX

height. Has been solo-reversed (more than once).
FSA Nick Buckley

According to folklore, Jon Biddle once attempted to jump into the sea from above *Freeborn Man*. He hit the slab and tore off his shorts, landing in the sea starkers.

Herman Borg's Basic Pulley Slippage   E5 6c **S1**   50 feet
A very eliminate line packed close to the left of *Freeborn Man*. Someone's got to solo it. [NYS]

Halcyon Days   E1 5a/b **S2**   50 feet
Best attempted when cruising at least E2. Start in the first sentry-box along the ledge to *The Conger*.
Climb the overhanging groove above and corner-crack above that. Safer in its second half, less ledge to hit.
FSA Unknown

The Musharagi Tree   E2 5c **S1**   50 feet
Either climb the arête left of *Halcyon Days* or start up *The Conger* and move up rightwards onto the slab. Both alternatives reach the steep corner above; then follow this to the top. Finish as for *Halcyon Days*.
FSA Jon Biddle/Jon Williams (1.8.88)

Swordfish Trombones   E5 6b **S2**   50 feet
[Photos p.32b] If you gotta the cojones!
Start up *The Conger*; then pull steeply up the groove above to a crack-system through the big roofs. Scrungey moves reach the lip of the roof (crux) and a finish on the ledge of *Jellied*. Respect is due to the FSA.
FSA Andy Donson (Summer 1995)

The Conger   E1 5c **S0/1**   60 feet
[Photo p.16d] Only the best route of all. Amenable, safe, and shockingly good, and the best possible introduction to deep water soloing. This route is easier to solo: it gets E2 if climbed using trad gear. Start in the second (smaller) of the two sentry-boxes found when traversing left along the ledge from *Helix*. Getting onto the route is the second hardest move. Pull into the slab corner and start traversing left across corners and arêtes until you come to the large peg-streaked block of the crux section. Pass this and the chimney beyond to a major jug-fest and finish by pulling left up a slab with flake jugs. Traditionally, you should now jump off the top.
FSA Nick Buckley (26.6.83)

Jellied   E3 5c **S1**   60 feet
One of the two variant finishes of *The Conger*. From the crux chimney go rightwards to finish on the nose of rock above. Friable holds and big splashdown potential.
FSA Jon Biddle (3.8.90)

CONNOR COVE
THE CONGER CAVE

JUMP/DIVE PLATFORM

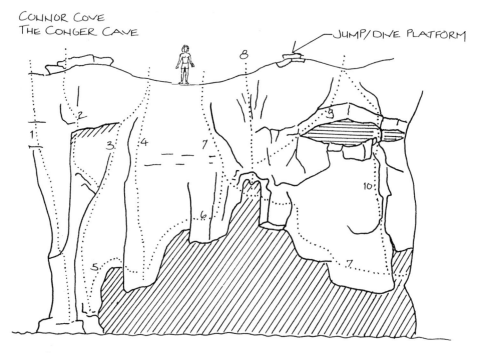

1 LEAP OF FAITH
2 TSUNAMI
3 A BRIDGE TOO FAR
4 FURIOUS PIG
5 JON WILLIAM'S TRAVERSE
6 THE GREAT SHARK HUNT
7 THE CONGER
8 SNAP, CRACKLE AND PLOP
9 JELLIED
10 SWORDFISH TROMBONES

Snap Crackle and Plop   E3 5c   **S1**   60 feet
From the crux chimney of *The Conger* go directly up the pocketed overhanging wall above. No good if you can't handle commitment.
FSA Dominic Cook (11.9.90)

The following six routes need access consideration. For both *Furious Pig* and *The Great Shark Hunt*, the best way to enjoy the route is with a bench seat lowered to the left-hand end of the pillar, which is completely undercut. On this you can sit comfortably, take off your harness, and pre-scope the moves. Then, when you're ready, pull onto the rock and away from the seat. For routes from *John Williams Traverse* to *Leap of Faith*, a bench seat would also work nicely. Alternatively, down-climb *A Bridge Too Far* if you're confident, or swim across from the base of *Helix* (boots and chalkbag on head). The ledges underneath *A Bridge Too Far* and *Leap of Faith* are large enough to sit and dry out on, swell permitting, before doing the solo.

The Great Shark Hunt   E4 6a   **S0**   40 feet
Swing onto the hanging pillar and move right immediately under roofs until you can pull steeply into an undercut groove (crux). Hands-off rest possible. Climb the groove to jugs and go right again to the edge of *The Conger*'s chimney; finish as for *The Conger*.
FSA Pete Oxley

Furious Pig   E2 5c   **S0**   40 feet
Once again onto the hanging pillar, but this time, up and left slightly to the top.
FSA Crispin Waddy (3.89)

A nice challenge with full S0 safety factor is to down-climb *Furious Pig* to the base of the hanging pillar, and then break rightwards to ascend *The Great Shark Hunt*. An awesome loop.

Jon Williams Traverse   XS 6a   **S0**   20/60 feet
Traverse onto the hanging pillar from *A Bridge Too Far*; then choose your destiny.
FSA Jon Williams (5.90)

A Bridge Too Far   Hard Very Severe 5b   **S2**   50 feet
The counter line to *The Conger*. Starting in the roof-capped groove/corner at the west edge of The Conger Cave, climb the corner to the roof and bridge rightwards across the chimney; finish to the right. Not entirely safe landings in the corner.
FSA Unknown

Tsunami   E4 6b   **S0/1**   60 feet
An excellent find, with a nice deep well underneath, but a highish crux.
Starting up *A Bridge Too Far*, follow the corner for 20 feet until a line of jug holds lead left onto the arête. Follow these; then pull up to a bulge and rock onto this on crimplies (crux). Finish directly above. Safe but scary. (An anagram of the name of

this route is 'I am nuts'.)
FSA Damian Cook (6.93)

Leap of Faith   E3 5c   **S2**   60 feet
Perfectly sound rock and beautiful climbing, except for the distracting spike sticking
out underneath.
Start on the sea-level ledge left of *A Bridge Too Far* corner. Climb directly up onto
the blunt arête and gradually left onto a crux on pockets through a fair old bulge.
Finish direct. Excitement fully guaranteed. Better to jump off than to fall.
FSA Damian Cook (6.93)

Dave Ardron on *Fathoms* Photo: Jon Biddle

The Funky Wall

The following routes are centred about 80 yards west of The Conger Cave, on the wall before the first huge cavern. Best found by locating a rusty stake 10 yards back from the cliff edge, only a few yards from where the rock pavement gives way to an earthy slope. Looking over the cliff, a 15-foot-long strip ledge can be seen about 15 feet above the sea. To access the routes, either abseil onto the ledge, or down-climb *The Rise and Dear Demise of the Funky Nomadic Tribes*. To exit the water after falling off any of the following routes, swim to the east (right) end of the ledge and scramble easily up to the ledge itself, where hopefully an ab-rope and ascending gear await you. If not, solo *The Rise and Dear Demise of the Funky Nomadic Tribes*, or swim back to *Helix*.

The Rise and Dear Demise of the Funky Nomadic Tribes
Hard Very Severe   5a   **S2/3**   40 feet
Not really a fall-off route, but OK to jump. Solid frictiony rock, and probably the best escape from this area when you're wet, especially if you have a shunt. Excellent edges, side-pulls and incuts lead direct up the shallow groove from the left end of the ledge; step rightwards to finish from the ledge at the top of the groove.
FSA The Cook Brothers (8.90)

Amazonia   E1   5b   **S0/1**   50 feet
Just left of The Funky Ledge is a second small ledge. Get onto this and move diagonally leftwards to a small arête and corner, which you climb on the left-hand side to the *Fathoms* ledge. Pleasantly straightforward and above deep water.
FSA Jonathan Cook (4.6.93)

Donald, Where's Your Trousers?   E1   5b   **S0/1**   40 feet
From The Funky Ledge, drop down and traverse left along the break for about 30 feet until you reach a small ledge underneath a diagonal leftward-leaning groove. From this ledge, step up and right out of the groove and go diagonally past undercuts to finish up a short layback flake to the ledge.
FSA Crispin Waddy (8.9.86)

Fathoms   E3   5c   **S0/1**   40 feet
[Photo p.32a] A special route, with a spectacular splashdown. Start as for *Donald Where's Your Trousers?*.
Follow the groove leftwards, which finishes with the biggest wrap-around jug there is. From this, crank up and rightwards (crux) to finish on a wide ledge, 10 feet below the cliff-top. Scramble easily out. Photogenic if someone abseils over the cliff edge to look down on the crux. Seek it out.
FSA Crispin Waddy (8.9.86)

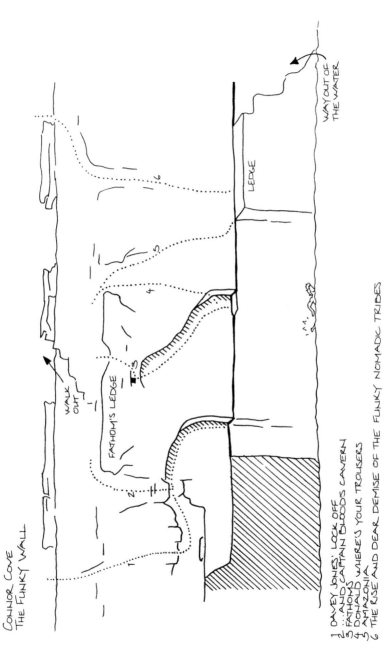

CONNOR COVE
THE FUNKY WALL

WAY OUT OF
THE WATER

LEDGE

WALK
OUT

FATHOM'S LEDGE

1 DAVEY JONES' LOCK OFF
2 ...AND CAPTAIN BLOODS CAVERN
3 FATHOMS
4 DONALD WHERE'S YOUR TROUSERS
5 AMAZONIA
6 THE RISE AND DEAR DEMISE OF THE FUNKY NOMADIC TRIBES

...And Captain Blood's Cavern   E3 6a **S1**   80 feet
[Photo p.48a] One of the three finest routes in the cove. Seepage usually dries out
by May. If you need inspiration, just check out the photo.
Traverse past *Fathoms*; pleasant jug-hauling brings you to a small corner before
the break turns into the huge cavern. You should now be underneath a
leftward-leading groove. Crank into the groove (crux) and undercut your way up
left until a rest is reached just before a bulge. Undercut into the bulge and reach
over onto large flat holds and haul up (second crux) to an excellent rest in a
groove. Relax for a minute and exit rightwards onto the *Fathoms* ledge.
FSA Jonathan Cook (8.8.90)

Davy Jones' Lock-off   E4 6a **S2**   90 feet
The highest of the Connor solos, so don't wear your best undies.
At the end of the leftward traverse of *...And Captain Blood's Cavern*. Instead of
pulling over the bulge (second crux), step downward and continue leftwards for 15
feet to an obvious jutting foot-ledge. Move up directly to undercuts and then pull
through the mild bulge on sidepulls and slopers to a massive shakeout. Go up
and vaguely left to finish. S2 as there are brittle final holds at 60 feet.
FSA Crispin Waddy (8.94)

Jumps/Dives

The Conger area has no shortage of ledges to throw yourself off, so if you want to catch some serious air, try the following in ascending order:

The small sloping stance 15 feet up *Helix*
The broad ledge at half height on *Helix* (25 to 30 feet)
The nose at the finish of *Jellied* (45 feet)
The top of *The Conger* (60 feet)
The Rio Point, the prow above *Helix* (about 60 feet) [Cover photo]

The Aerial Runway

Fixings are in place above *Leap of Faith* and at the base of *Helix*. Best done using a static rope. Clip a pulley onto the rope, and a karabiner and short sling onto that, then launch out. Fast and furious and best one person per pulley, as two lads once proved.

The Parachute

An invention of Dominic Cook. Produced from a car cover, some string and a couple of broom handles; Blue Peter would be proud of this creation. It has been used quite successfully from the top of The Conger Cave, and slightly less so from the top of *Benny* (though it must have had some effect merely to have a dislocated shoulder falling from 90 feet into only 2 feet of water).

Dancing Ledge West Zawn

A daunting solo venue. Compares to a drive up the M1 in a *Citroen 2CV*. Atmospheric in the extreme. Most sport climbers never seem to venture down here, despite the superb quality and character of the routes.

For those familiar with the quarried walls at the back of the ledge, this is nothing like it. Only recently developed as a solo venue, when a far-sighted (or short-brained) Robertson stumbled upon its potential at the end of the frenzied 1995 season.

Approach From Wareham

Follow the A351 south. As you are leaving the historic town of Corfe Castle, turn right towards Langton Matravers. This road climbs a steep hill and then follows a ridge, before descending into Langton Matravers. About 200 yards after passing a small shop on the left, turn right into Durnford Drive. Follow this road, which becomes a rough track, to a parking-area at the bottom of a field.

Leave your car here and walk south, past Spyway Farm and across two fields until you reach the top of a steep hill. Dancing Ledge is at the bottom.

The back walls of the main quarry are extremely popular with sport climbers. The slabby walls on the lower ledge are equally popular with beginners. In the summer this area is excellent for family picnics and swimming. Keep this in mind if you like an audience.

General

Dancing Ledge has some excellent bouldering potential, both on the lower ledges in the form of long traverses, and on the back wall, especially in the western back corner around the bricked-up cave.

The sea-level ledges have some excellent getting-wave-trashed potential, if you're into wave abuse. Take care and wear a wet suit. The enclosed corners and gullies give the best value.

Any jumping? Of course there is. Try stepping off the top of *Here Comes the Hizbollah*, but take care of the boulders further out – keep in tight. The west side of the next zawn, to the east, is also fine. High tide recommended for both.

For the West Zawn, follow the steep path onto the floor of the quarry, and bear rightwards. Trace the cliff edge westwards for about 40 yards. There is a well-hidden staple bolt near the cliff edge, on the eastern edge of the large zawn. Abseil from here, for 25 feet to a good ledge and a single belay bolt.

Here Comes the Hizbollah   E2 5c/6a   (6b+)   **S2**   30 feet

A short steep climb, starting from the ledge by the belay bolt.
Simply power through the overhangs above, and don't fall off before the first roof.

The upper crux section is totally safe.
FSA Mike Robertson (24.9.95)

Lucretia, My Reflection   E3 6a   (6c)   **S0/1**   40 feet
[Photo p.48b] An excellent solo, with very varied climbing.
From the overhung corner, gain the hanging slab with difficulty, and scrunge onto it (easier for the short). Traverse leftwards until sloping jugs show the way to the top; a 5c move here makes you think. A classic solo situation, and an essential tick. Good water throughout.
FSA Mike Robertson (24.9.95)

FYB   E3 6a   (6c)   **S1**   35 feet
This is the line between the previous two routes.
Perform the *Lucretia, My Reflection* start (crux) and get a nice rest. Traverse rightwards along the break (keeping an eye on the ledge below) and then pounce up and leftwards to good holds (and safe territory). Continue on spaced jugs to the top. A pleasant neighbour to *Lucretia, My Reflection*.
FSA Mike Robertson (7.10.95)

The Pump Will Tear Us Apart   E5 6b   (7a+)   **S2/3**   50 feet
A superb and inspiring line, probing the very depths of the zawn. A classic frightener which looks a great deal more dangerous than it is.
Power out confidently along the obvious low break-line, whilst keenly observing the boulders lurking discreetly below. Press on to a useful rest by the second thread runner, after which the crux roof section is despatched via some hideously inverted moves and powerful reaches. Continue past a large flake, and climb direct to the top, exiting slightly rightwards. Note that the entire crux section and the top wall are fortuitously situated above a good pool, between a pretty group of boulders. Have fun and be scared.
FSA Mike Robertson (29.9.95)

Mariner's Graveyard (Reverse of first pitch)   XS 6a   (7a)   **S3**   50 feet
You guessed it, this one really does get the death-on-a-stick label. On the zawn junkies' list, so it enters this guide as an unrealized solo. Listen carefully, children. The ever-so-correct line of *Mariner's Graveyard* follows the break-line as for the last route, but stays with it all the way to the square-cut ledge in the middle of the zawn.
Pitch 2 climbs the leaning headwall above. But forget that.
Abseil down the second pitch, jettison your harness, psyche yourself silly and reverse the first pitch. Why? Means you get the scary section done while you're fresh, leaving the 'pumped senseless' section for the 'fairly safe as long as you fall outwards properly' landing-zone. Inspired? Me too. A pint of beer or a small parachute could help on this potential epic. Big tides only, kids. Serious and committing. [NYS]

Lulworth Cove

If you ever studied Geography or Geology at school, then you will have heard of this place. Stair Hole has some of the best examples of synclines and anticlines in the country. In fact, it is such a phenomenon that we have to thank for the remarkably steep routes hereabouts.

This place has the hardest deep water solos in the county. So far, routes of F7b+ and F7c have fallen in the search to push the limits. There are routes of F7c+ and F8a which could be soloed here; they are just waiting for someone with the strength and 'cojones' to do them.

The atmosphere here is very seaside-like: plenty of cafes, pubs, and little shops. The beach in the main Lulworth Cove is usually packed in the school holidays and can seem very picturesque when there are yachts moored in this natural harbour. The proximity of all of these touristy attractions makes it an obvious family venue, with plenty for all to do.

When soloing routes on the seaward side of Stair Hole, you are only 10 yards from the pebble beach. If you are about to fall off, check below for oblivious swimmers and scuba divers, as they can hardly be expected to look out for you.

Introduction

This area has been used by climbers sporadically for the last 30 years. The steep sea cliffs East of Stair Hole are littered with VS and HVS routes, all with ice-axe finishes up the steep grass slopes. None of these routes has had more than two or three ascents and they are for the epic-seeking climber only. These, for obvious reasons, are not described.

In 1987 Pete Oxley came along and climbed the ground-breaking Mark of the Beast, on traditional gear. After some thought he gave the route E7 for an on-sight attempt, making it one of the hardest routes in the south at the time. Two other steep routes were climbed on the same day. Things went quiet again.

In 1991 the Cook brothers were attracted to the scene, and they set their minds to repeating the routes hereabouts. Soon, they became bored with the hassle of carrying ropes and gear to the base of these routes and started soloing them. Early successes at Connor Cove had given them the confidence that they could solo just as hard as they could lead, so they went to work on existing routes and new lines.

Now there are more routes which were first soloed than those which were first climbed using bolts or traditional gear. Mark of the Beast has been soloed a number of times by Oxley. Horny L'il Devil has had dozens of solo ascents (and splashdowns). Only two of the bolt routes which are justifiably soloable await solo ascents. Stair Hole has become the soloing venue. A summer weekend may see as many as a dozen people soloing in and around the caves in relative safety. This must be an ideal area to

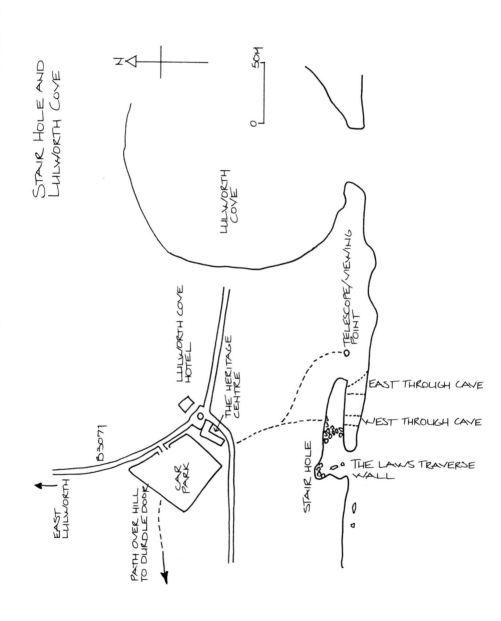

STAIR HOLE AND
LULWORTH COVE

N

0   50M

LULWORTH
COVE

LULWORTH COVE
HOTEL

THE HERITAGE
CENTRE

B3071

EAST
LULWORTH

CAR
PARK

PATH OVER HILL
TO DURDLE DOOR

TELESCOPE/VIEWING
POINT

EAST THROUGH CAVE

WEST THROUGH CAVE

THE LAWS TRAVERSE
WALL

STAIR HOLE

practise your skills; so learn to swim if you have to and get down there and join in the fun.

Note. Currently, the landowner (The Weld Estate) does not wish anyone to climb here. It is hoped that in the future some form of agreement can be reached. Watch the climbing press for details. Meanwhile, **please honour this restriction**.

Approach
The nearest towns to Lulworth are Wool and Wareham. From the A352, which links these two towns, Lulworth Cove is very well signposted. The main car-park is a little pricey, at £3 for a full day in the summer. However, this does give you a mere 2-minute walk-in to the crag and the beach.

To get to the climbing, follow the gravel path from the road at the south-east corner of the large car-park, i.e. the one which leads directly south from the small Coastguard garage with the blue door, over a small hill. After 30 yards, Stair Hole comes into view, at the bottom of a steep slope. You are faced by a large slab, breached by two obvious caves, with an entrance out to sea on the right. Before the slab, there is a pebble beach. At most tides there is a small spit of pebbles from the base of the steep slope over to the base of the slab.

The seaward side of this slab is where most of the action lies, out of sight of the holiday-makers and geologists on the pebble beach. Scramble up the slab from the pebbles, taking care not to attract any holiday-makers, to the ridge at the top. This is where access to most of the routes is described from.

Aspect
The majority of routes are south-facing. On any normal crag this would mean that you would see the sun for most of the day. However, the crag is so steep, that at midday in the summer, most routes are in the shade. This is not a problem, since in the summer it is usually so hot on the coast that you want to climb in the shade anyway. Stay on the beach if you want a tan!

Rough seas may also play havoc with your arrangements. Even on the sunniest of days, a strong wind can whip the up sea into a frenzy of waves topped with white horses. This is not the best time to go soloing: the routes may get wet and big waves have the power of the Atlantic behind them. As a rough guide, if the swell (height between top and bottom of waves) is more than a couple of feet, stick only to those routes you know you can flash. If the swell is more than three or four feet, shelve your soloing ambitions for the day and retire to *The Castle Inn* in East Lulworth (or go bolt climbing on Portland).

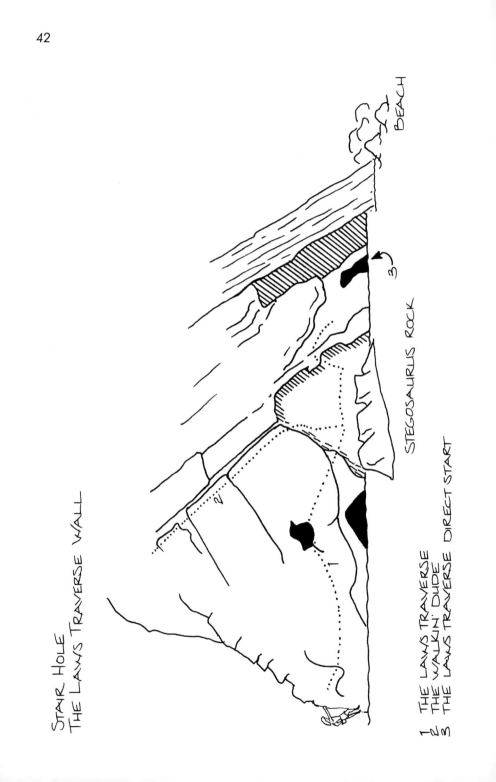

STAIR HOLE
THE LAWS TRAVERSE WALL

BEACH

STEGOSAURUS ROCK

1 THE LAWS TRAVERSE
2 THE WALKIN' DUDE
3 THE LAWS TRAVERSE DIRECT START

Stair Hole Entrance

The Laws Traverse   XS 6a   **S0**   50 feet
[Photo p.64a] A total classic due to its perfect rock, brilliant moves, and proximity to the sea (never more than 6 feet below). A must for any competent party. The race for the first ascent involved four climbers all jockeying for position and trying to summon up the bottle to commit to the starting-roof. But that's all history now. This traverse provides an excellent opportunity for posing, especially the first few moves across the roof. Photo opportunities are plentiful.
If the tide allows, walk over to the hanging slab on the west side of the Stair Hole entrance. If the tide is high, it becomes necessary either to wade across a small inlet, or to traverse (on jugs) around it.
From the slab, swing around to its underside onto an obvious jutting jug and ape across the roof to the safety of a large boulder in the back of the cave. This gives a chance to let the adrenaline rush subside a little. Then traverse towards the open sea on good holds all the way to the arête, spurning the rest in the half-way cave (if you wish). Got there? Well, turn around and reverse it: that's the way back.
FSA Pete Oxley (29.5.93)

There is a variation on this route which requires a low tide. When traversing after the large boulder, ensure you remain only just above the water line. More sustained than the original.

Laws Direct Start   XS 6b   **S0**   15 feet
Another variation is the direct start. This cunningly sneaks through the cramped archway, using hideous slopers, to arrive (with an element of luck) on the big rounded boulder. So low above the sea, it can be treated as a boulder-problem, albeit with a 'wet legs' potential. Desperate.
FSA Mike Robertson (5.7.95)

The Walkin' Dude   XS 6a.   **S3**   40 feet
Originally thought to be a chop route, but a spring-tide showed that it could be less than lethal for the second ascent. It is S3 even on a regular high tide. Even at high spring-tide, there are submerged boulders lurking down there.
Start as for *The Laws Traverse*. From the boulder at the back of the cave, follow *The Laws Traverse* for 5 feet; then climb the wall above. This soon leads to a leftward-leaning ramp. Climb this to its culmination. Slightly dubious-looking rock, with a fairly high crux. The 6a bit is the starting roof on *The Laws Traverse*. The meat of this route is only 5b/c, but feels much harder.
FSA Mike Robertson (26.6.93)

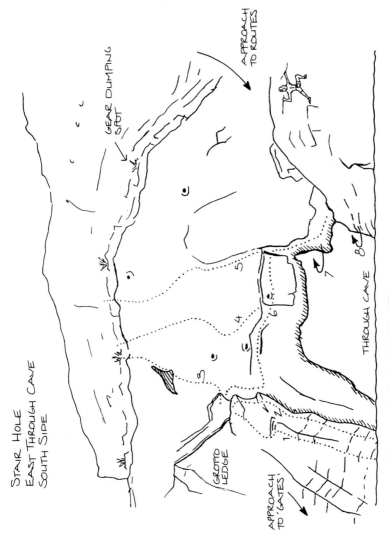

STAIR HOLE
EAST THROUGH CAVE
SOUTH SIDE

GEAR DUMPING SPOT

APPROACH TO ROUTES

GROTTO LEDGE

APPROACH TO 'GATES'

THROUGH CAVE

1 CAPTAIN BASTARD GOT THEIR FIRST
2 ANARCHY STAMPEDE
3 STAGEDIVIN'
4 ANDRENOCHROME
5 THE MARK OF THE BEAST
6 HORNY 'LIL DEVIL
7 SLIDING DOWN THE BANNISTER
8 LEVIATHAN FLOP

The East Cave

This is the cave which has the greatest number of bolted routes, and it contains some of the best steep climbing in the country. All of the climbing is on the 40-degree overhanging seaward face, an imposing venue. You *must* be very fit to enjoy this area, or enjoy swimming a lot.

The main features of this cliff are the slab at the foot of the eastern side, and the short steep wall, topped by a large ledge (The Grotto) at the western side.

To get to the slab at the foot of the eastern side, approach from the ridge. Walking eastwards along the ridge, you pass an awkward slab just before reaching a pillar. Skirt this to the right to reach the gear dump spot 15 feet further on. Once you have changed, carry on in the same direction; you will very soon be scrambling. Descend gradually in an easterly direction for 30 feet, until it is possible to climb down a short groove onto the slab below. You can now traverse back leftwards underneath the left side of the impressive roof.

To get to The Grotto, approach as above until you reach the pillar. From this point, down-climb towards the sea on large holds for about 20 feet, until you reach the spacious ledge. These approaches are a little daunting the first time, but are only V Diff.

Sliding down the Banister   XS 6a   **S0**   15 feet
This route gets from the seaward side of the cave to the landward side, about 6 feet above the water, skirting the hanging prow under *Horny L'il Devil*.
Start underneath *Mark of the Beast*. Climb through the arch toward the pebble beach, staying just underneath the roof.
FSA Pete Oxley (23.5.92)

Does Leviathan Plop Float?   XS 5c   **S0**   15 feet
This short problem gets from the seaward side of the cave to the landward.
Start underneath *Mark of the Beast*. Squirm and power your way under the arch, staying only a couple of feet above the water.
FSA Damian Cook (7.91)

Horny L'il Devil   E4 6a   (7a)   **S0**   35 feet
[Photos p.48d and rear cover] Another Lulworth classic. Fantastic climbing in an amazing situation. All of the holds on this route are jugs, but they are well spaced, the wall is 40 degrees overhanging, and the footholds are fairly small. The route traverses the base of the main face from right to left. It is safe at all tides and reaches a maximum of 15 feet above the sea. A bit like *The Conger* really, but much harder. There are bolts on the route if you want to practise it first.
Start underneath *Mark of the Beast*. Make two moves up to the obvious break and follow this on excellent holds to the other side of the roof. Tricky moves up and left land you on the safe haven of The Grotto.
This route gets easier with practice. There are a few trick moves, mostly reach-throughs. There is also a spectacular hands-off rest at the small recess.

It is possible to do the route left to right. This makes some moves harder, and some moves easier. Overall, this is a little harder and more daunting as you would fall onto rock on the last two moves.
FSA Pete Oxley (Summer 1993)

Mark of the Beast   E6 6b   (7c)   **S1**   45 feet
[Photo p.48d] A fantastic route, and it's soloable (by those with the ability). It takes the weakness in the centre of the face. Probably best worked on a rope, since it is very hard, with the crux being a large reach right at the top. Several Sheffield hopefuls have failed even to redpoint this route.
Only one person has soloed this route so far, that being the first ascensionist himself.
Start from the leftmost side of the slab. A couple of easy moves into a chimney lead you on to well spaced, good holds. The crux is the last couple of moves 35 feet above deep water. It is likely you will be pumped when you get here, and these moves require total commitment.
FSA Pete Oxley (Summer 1993)

Adrenachrome   E7 6c   (8a)   **S1**   45 feet
Another hard classic on this face. When (if) this is soloed, it will be a major achievement. The crux is dynamic, so landings should be OK. All of the climbing is above water.
Follow *Horny L'il Devil* for 15 feet (to the upside-down rest); then dyno upwards, fairly direct, to the top. [NYS]

Stagedivin'   E4 6b   (7a+)   **S1**   25 feet
This has had a couple of on-sight solo ascents now. The climbing is quite powerful and it is pumpy, despite being only 20 feet long. Very committing as it starts 25 feet up.
Start from The Grotto and climb diagonally rightwards to the top. A spotter may be required for the first couple of moves to prevent falling back onto The Grotto.
FSA Pete Oxley (Summer 1993)

Captain Bastard Got There First   XS 5c   **S0**   25 feet
Scramble down a groove from the south-west corner of the grotto (Severe), and then traverse right for 10 feet just above the water. Just before the traverse reaches a blunt arête, this route climbs the groove above, back onto The Grotto ledge. Quite committing.
FSA Jonathan Cook (21.7.91)

The Anarchy Stampede   XS 6a   **S0**   25 feet
Much steeper than it looks from the other side of the cave.
Where the previous route starts up, traverse right for a couple of moves and climb the steep wall, initially on poor holds, then on jugs to The Grotto.
FSA Jon Biddle (6.9.88)

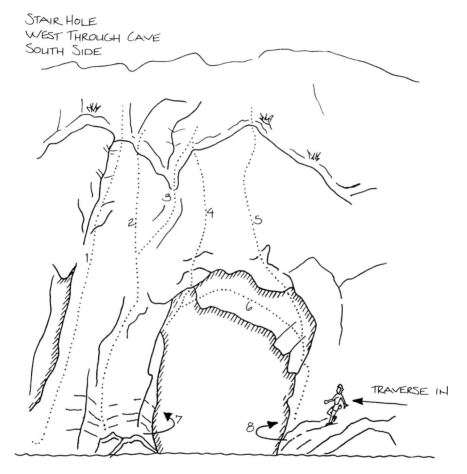

STAIR HOLE
WEST THROUGH CAVE
SOUTH SIDE

TRAVERSE IN

1 THE RAGGAMUFFIN WAY
2 CRAZY NOTION
3 ANIMAL MAGNETISM
4 NEVER KNEEL TO SKELETOR
5 GATES OF GREYSKULL
6 MEET HERBERT THE TURBOT TONIGHT
7 THE MAYPOLE
8 LAST SEASON'S LOOZAS

The West Cave

Although this cave only has three bolted routes, there are plenty of solos to be done, some at a pleasantly amenable grade. The first route to be described is also the longest.

The Maypole   XS 5b   **S0**   250 feet
This route traverses from the pebble beach, round to the sea, and back through The West Cave onto the beach. The tourists will wonder how you managed to stay dry. A good introduction to the traversing hereabouts, and has some decent posing value too.
Start on the pebble beach on the landward side of Stair Hole. Traverse the eastern side of the entrance to Stair Hole just above the water-line, generally on easy ground. Keep going into The West Cave. Things get a little interesting now. Drop down until your feet are almost in the water and make some long stretches between good holds until a prominent flake crack is reached. You now have a choice:
1. keep going at this level until you are through the cave and onto the beach;
2. climb the flake onto a hanging slab, scramble across this, then drop down to a ledge just above the sea to join option 1.
Option 1 is quite pumpy, but you drop only a couple of feet if you come off. Option 2 is easier, but the drop to the sea is more like 15 feet. Make your mind up. A word of caution: only pussies take Option 2.
FSA Jon Williams (23.5.90)

Truth, Justice and the Ragamuffin Way   E2 5b   **S1**   50 feet
This route has a scary crux, well above the water, with a friable finish. Not for the faint-hearted.
Follow *The Maypole* past the easy section (i.e. for about 150 feet). Make an awkward step around a sharp arête. You will now see a deep black groove above you (**don't** climb this, it's incredibly unpleasant and isn't above deep water anyway). The route takes the wall and hanging V-groove 10 feet to the right. The crux is entering the hanging groove, about 30 feet up. Once in the groove, climb diagonally rightwards across slightly fragile rock. Take care, it's a long way down.
FSA Jon Biddle (20.7.91)

Crazy Notion   E4 6b   **S1**   40 feet
The hardest route here to be climbed solo on the first ascent.
Climb *Animal Magnetism* to the second bolt; then spurn the line of chalked-up holds to the right and climb the overhanging wall straight above, exiting slightly leftwards.
FSA Mike Robertson (22.8.95)

Animal Magnetism   E5 6b   (7a+)   **S1**   40 feet
[Photo p.64] This FSA showed the way ahead for mere mortals at Lulworth Cove. Not on-sighted yet. A couple of hidden holds on this steep route are the key to success, which is why it is so difficult to flash. Also, it remains hard even after the crux.

Dominic Cook on 'And Captain Cook's Cavern' Photo: Jonathan Cook

Mike Robertson on *Lucretia* Photo: Jonathan Cook

Joff Cook on *The Gates of Greyskull* Photo: Steve Taylor

Follow *The Maypole* until it reaches the entrance to The West Cave. *Animal Magnetism* blasts up the rightward leaning groove line above you. Be warned – it finishes on large slopers.
FSA Jonathan Cook (7.94)

Never Kneel to Skeletor   E6 6c   (7c+)   **S1**   40 feet
The hardest route in this cave. Extremely technical and very, very steep. Its upside-down nature and very committing moves mean that an awkward landing is possible.
Traverse directly into The West Cave from the beach and climb up onto the hanging slab to a two-bolt belay. From its left-hand side, launch out along the line of bolts across what can only be described as a roof. Eventually, this route joins *Animal Magnetism* for its last move, where the difficulties relent by an order of magnitude. [NYS]

Herbert the Turbot   XS 6b   **S1**   30 feet
This route has baffled would-be second ascensionists for years now.
From the start of *Never Kneel to Skeletor*, somehow get onto the hanging slab across the yawning gap. Traverse the slab rightwards to the start of *The Gates of Greyskull*. The last few moves are a little dodgy, as there is a risk of hitting rock if you should fall off.
FSA Jon Biddle (22.7.91)

The Gates of Greyskull   E6 6b   (7b+)   **S1**   45 feet
[Photo p.48c] A fantastic outing on good holds. It takes the bolted line up the middle of the very overhanging face above The West Cave.
Scramble down to the eastern side of the seaward entrance of The West Cave. *Last Season's Loozas* will get you there, but takes ages. It is possible to abseil in fairly direct, past a bolt to keep you in line, once you know your way around. From the slab, launch up and left onto the roof and climb to its triangular apex pretty much directly. The crux is a blind slap around the lip of the roof, to a hidden slot on the slab above. This route is quite difficult to work on the lead because of the angle, so why not go for the on-sight?
FSA Jonathan Cook (14.8.95)

Last Season's Loozas   Hard Very Severe 5a   **S0/1**   200 feet
Another long traverse. Some sections are quite easy and getting wet is likely even in calm seas.
From The Grotto ledge in The East Cave, descend to sea-level. Start traversing leftwards past various arêtes and deep grooves until you reach the entrance to The West Cave. Step around into the cave and then follow the ramp up into the roof of the cave, where it gets darker all the way. When the ramp ends, descend the opposite side in a constricting chimney, almost to sea-level, where it is possible to exit through the rock window overlooking the beach.
FSA The Cook Brothers (21.7.91)

The chimney mentioned above reaches all the way through to The East Cave. When the sea is calm and the tide quite low, you can swim through this cleft. Slightly rougher seas and higher tides make the trip more interesting up to a point where it becomes either impossible or lethal. Obviously, the trip is possible in both directions. Not recommended for claustrophobics or those of a nervous disposition.

Problems inside The West Cave

The back wall of The West Cave has yielded a number of difficult solos/boulder-problems in recent times. This wall is now criss-crossed by a number of very difficult problems, all climbed on-sight, usually after a number of splashdowns. Before attempting these problems, check that:

you have a spotter, if required;
no-one is going to swim underneath at the crucial point;
you have marked likely holds with your chalking stick.

These problems are all described as if you are looking at the wall from inside the cave.

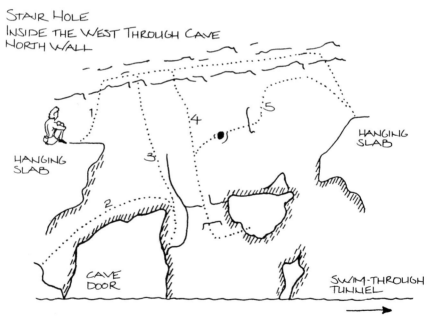

1 ROUTE 66
2 ESCOBAR
3 CONTORTIONS
4 SHOWTIME
5 EL GUAPO

Route 66   XS 5b **S1**   40 feet
This one gets high quickly and is therefore a bit scary. Compensation comes in the way of large holds and bridging/crawling once up in the roof. The line taken is the obvious traverse in the roof of the cave. The crux is the series of moves off the hanging slab – it is advisable to employ the services of a spotter.
From the hanging slab, climb up onto the traverse-line and go rightwards until you reach the other side of the cave. Climb down the latter part of *Last Season's Loozas* to finish.
FSA Mike Robertson (30.7.94)

Escobar   E4 6b **S0**   20 feet
Take the line from the lower left-hand side of the wall, over the lip of the main entrance, then down onto a small ledge on the right-hand side of the main entrance. Some very committing long reaches required.
FSA Jonathan Cook (1.8.95)

Contortions   E4 6b **S1**   30 feet
A continuation to *Escobar*.
From the finishing ledge of *Escobar*, climb directly upwards on good holds (but steep rock), eventually reaching the traverse of *Route 66*. A spotter on the hanging slab gives confidence for the last moves to get to a large slot on *Route 66*.
FSA Mike Robertson (1.8.95)

Showtime   E4 6b **S1**   25 feet
Very reachy and powerful. Scramble into the cave through the window.
Step down and left underneath the steep pillar. Take a deep breath and commit yourself to some very hard moves above deep water. If you are lucky enough to get to the top, traverse left along *Route 66* and either down-climb onto the left hanging slab or jump into the sea. Spotter advised.
FSA Jonathan Cook (5.8.95)

Much better is:

El Guapo   E5 6b **S0**   25 feet
A variation finish to *Showtime* and certainly harder. First ascent was fully on-sight, following several splashdowns.
From half-way up *Showtime*, you can reach rightwards to a tree hole. Swing rightwards again to a flake jug and continue up and rightwards to the hanging slab.
FSA Jonathan Cook (19.9.95)

Lower than Whale Shit   XS 6b **S0**   30 feet
The sea-level traverse of the eastern wall inside the cave, from left to right. Far harder than it looks. Almost impossible to keep your feet dry except in calm seas and at low tide.
FSA Damian Cook/Gideon Fitch (8.95)

Other problems

There is an easy traverse around the pillar of *Showtime*. It goes at the same grade in either direction (VS 4c) and is a straightforward S0.

One can hand-traverse the lip of the arch taken by *Escobar*, but on the landward side. The holds are not that good, except for a hidden pocket which you can find for yourself. It goes at E3 6a S0. This is the only hard problem in full view of the beach.

No-one has done it yet, but it is possible to link *Escobar, Contortions, Showtime*, and *El Guapo*, without dropping onto the finishing ledge of *Escobar*. The ultimate grade should be E6 6b. Joff Cook is working on it, but it could take some time. Why not nip in and beat him to it?

Durdle Door

The venue you may have already ticked on foot with your loved one. Sadness aside, there's also some soloing potential. Read on…

Famous quotes about Durdle Door:

'Climbers will undoubtedly spoil the tourists' camera shots of this important feature.' (Heritage Coast spokesman, 1994)

'But what about the ice-cream van? It's noisy and it's ugly.' (Scott Titt, 1994)

'Yes, it's pretty. Let's use it for the video.' (Cliff Richard, 1991)

'I think I'll perform a double back twist flip swan dive off it.' (Nigel Rendell, December 1989)

Approach

Durdle Door is a large, natural limestone arch about a mile west of Lulworth Cove. It is well signposted from the minor road between Winfrith Newburgh and West Lulworth. Tourist pay about £2 in the summer to park behind a caravan-park, shortening the walk-in by about 10 minutes. It is also possible to park on the road and walk through the caravan-park.

Most routes should be accessed via abseil from the top of the arch. A path leads to the top of the arch, including a bit of scrambling. Please don't encourage tourists to follow you. Abseil from a block near the apex of the arch down its landward side to a small ledge 6 feet above the sea for routes on the outer leg. For routes on the inner leg, abseil down the seaward side of the arch or traverse in from the beach.

Note: Durdle Door is part of The Weld Estate. Please honour the **restriction** described on page 42.

To the climbing:

Sardine Liberation Front   E2 5c   **S1**   80 feet
The original deep water solo here, and still the most amenable. Unfortunately later incorporated into the lower section of *Riding to Babylon*, but still an excellent route in its own right.
It climbs the hanging arête on the inside of the arch, which is reached by a traverse in from the beach. Climb the seaward side of the arête to a sloping ledge. Make a long reach leftwards to jug on the arête; swing out and up to finish easily rightwards up the slab and cracks. A much easier scramble takes you to the top.
FSA Andy Donson (2.7.89)

The next two bolted routes require care regarding water depth and height. Observe that the water under the arch is significantly deeper in the middle. Check it carefully. A high or spring-tide is essential. On a more positive note, the top of the arch has been successfully jumped. Both routes are around 80 feet high.

Riding to Babylon   E5 6a   (7a+)   **S3**   75 feet
This takes the meat of *Sardine Liberation Front*, and then trends leftwards up the leaning headwall. After the crux, gaining the headwall, the biggest downer is the second crux, just below the top, reckoned to be about 70-75 feet above the sea. Food for thought, obviously graded S3 for the height, but above quite good water (on a good high tide) where it counts, below the upper section. If you climb F8b, you'll be fine. If, like us mere mortals, you don't get anywhere near F8s, you'll probably shit yourself. [NYS]

Arcwelder   E5 6b   (7b)   **S3**   75 feet
The counter line to *Riding to Babylon*, taking the seaward side of the inner arch, with a low crux. Check your landing here most carefully. If you're successful on the crux, don't stop until you reach the top. If you bag this, please send the authors a photo – you may well have beaten us to it. Brown lycra recommended. [NYS]

54

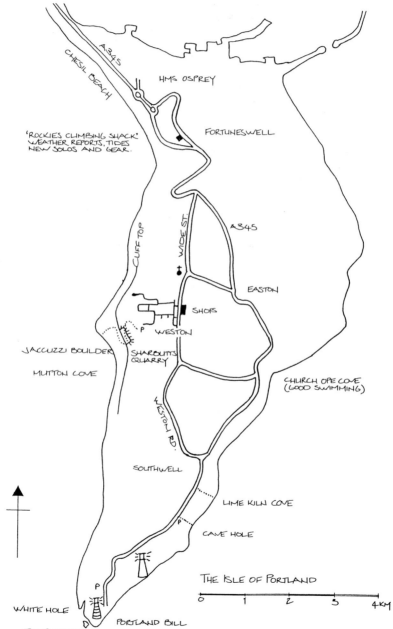

'ROCKIES CLIMBING SHACK'
WEATHER REPORTS, TIDES
NEW SOLOS AND GEAR.

CHESIL BEACH

A345

HMS OSPREY

FORTUNESWELL

CLIFF TOP

WIDE ST.

A345

EASTON

SHOPS

WESTON

JACCUZZI BOULDER

SHARBUTTS QUARRY

MUTTON COVE

CHURCH OPE COVE
(GOOD SWIMMING)

WESTON RD.

SOUTHWELL

LIME KILN COVE

CAVE HOLE

THE ISLE OF PORTLAND

0   1   2   3   4 KM

WHITE HOLE

PORTLAND BILL

THE PULPIT ROCK

Portland

Portland is not really an island, but a peninsula connected to the mainland Dorset town of Weymouth by a narrow spit of pebbles. This feature is known as Chesil Beach and provides access to the highest concentration of solo routes in this guide. The approach to each section is described from the top of the island plateau, where the steep zig-zag road levels out at *The Portland Heights Hotel*.

Here is a quick summary of the venues available:

Cave Hole
The overhead topos should be self-explanatory. The dotted lines wandering all over the place are in fact caves. Plenty of man-made features should mean you'll find your way around fairly easily. Please respect the Cave Hole area particularly, and carry out any litter you find. We climbers need to set an example. The area is diverse, exciting, and atmospheric. The premier sometimes-deep-water solo venue! A huge selection of differing routes. Home of *Crab Party* and *Octopus Weed*, two of the best roof solos anywhere. Much safer than *Separate Reality*! Another essential tick is the *Big Easy/Ixtlan* combination – don't miss it. Also great swimming and canoeing at the 'Hole'.

Lime Kiln Cave
A less intimidating area. Excellent if you want to 'clip' the routes first. Can be jumped at high tide. *The Bellybutton Traverse* and *Bay of Rainbows* are essential ticks. However, routes based upon *The Great Escape/Esmerelda's Monkey* are a far more serious proposition.

White Hole
Very intimidating and fluttery. Even the locals get scared here! High, technical cruxes, iffy water, very atmospheric. An excellent, long swim into Coastguard South.

Jacuzzi Boulder
Superb on a hot summer day at mid tide, low swell. Good swimming, even better (nude) sunbathing!

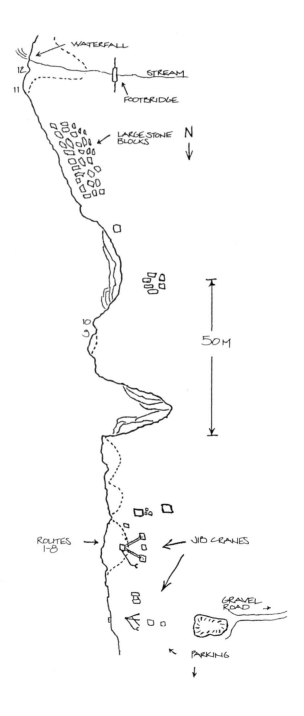

CAVE HOLE
TOPO A

Cave Hole

Approach

From *The Portland Heights Hotel,* head south down either the west or the east side of Portland, i.e. through either Weston or Easton. These two routes converge at *The Eight Kings Inn* in Southwell. Next to the pub is a road heading south (B3154), signposted to Portland Bill.

Drive down this road for approximately half a mile, at which point two cranes can be seen, at the bottom of fields to the left. Turn left down the gravel track marked 'Public Footpath' to the twin cranes. All Cave Hole routes are located in the caves starting at, and continuing south from, the cranes, which themselves are marked on the first overhead topo. The overhead topos (pages 56, 60, 62, and 69) are marked A, B, C, and D and are sequential, heading southwards; the numbers in brackets after the route names correspond to the numbers on these topos.

Routes are described from arrival at the two jib cranes.

Twenty-five feet from the more southerly of the two cranes is a large round rusty stake driven into a ledge. Down-climb the groove 6 feet to the north of this at Severe. This brings you to the southern end of Octopus Weed Cave. The entrance of the cave can be partially viewed from the stake ledge.

The Lip Traverse   XS 5b   **S0**   20 feet   (1)
Traverse the first half of the lip of Octopus Weed Cave, starting from the left side (looking in). All moves are feet off, but the handholds are large.
FSA Dominic Cook (16.8.95)

Magician's Trap   XS 6a/b   **S0**   15 feet   (2)
A continuation to the feet-off traverse of the left-hand side of the cave. Can be started separately. Drop down over the lip and make powerful, bunched moves rightwards under the jutting roof to emerge 10 feet further back onto the ledge above the cave.
FSA Dominic Cook (9.95)

Purple Shorts   XS 5a/5b   **S0**   20 feet   (3)
[Photo p.80d] The traverse onto the rather quaint rock bridge. Difficulty depends on how far you traverse rightwards before you bottle it and mantel!
FSA Guy Dixon (8.5.95)

Octopus Weed   XS 6a   **S0**   25 feet   (4)
[Photo p.80a] From the southern end of the above ledge/bridge/suspended platform/plank, hang backwards and launch yourself into a series of hanging heelhooks across a line of slots and jugs until a welcome foot-ledge on the far side is reached. Fantastic climbing, esoteric, a brilliant find. Try it footless, or even clothesless! An essential tick.
FSA Damian Cook (8.5.95)

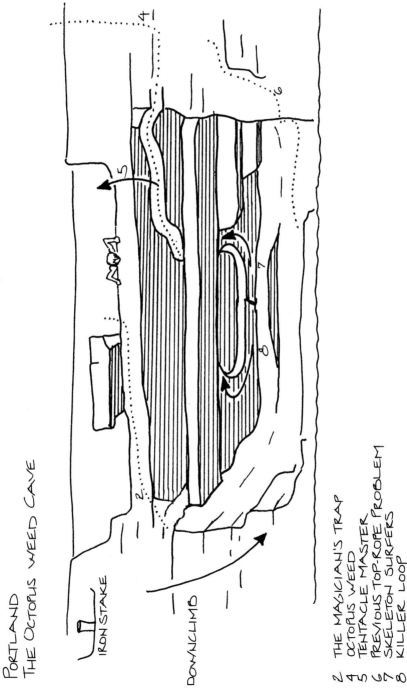

PORTLAND
THE OCTOPUS WEED CAVE

IRON STAKE

DOWNCLIMB

2 THE MAGICIAN'S TRAP
4 OCTOPUS WEED
5 TENTACLE MASTER
6 PREVIOUS TOP-ROPE PROBLEM
7 SKELETON SURFERS
8 KILLER LOOP

Tentacle Master XS 6b **S0** 20 feet (5)
Joff's desperate boulder-problem above good water. Climb *Octopus Weed* to the
protruding jug and then launch for a slopy side-pull; slap again for another,
slightly better sloper. One more lunge gains better holds. Two dramatic
splashdowns before successful first ascent!
FSA Jonathan Cook (27.7.95)

Previous Top-Rope Problem XS 5b **S0** 40 feet (6)
The low-level traverse of Octopus Weed Cave. A fun outing, variable according to
water depth/how much your chalk bag gets splashed. (Yes, that low!!)
FSA Damian Cook (8.5.95)

The following two routes are reached by walking to the back of the cave, along the
ledge until it ends. Above are two shelf/roof cracks. Their starts are shared reaching
up to the ceiling at the end of the ledge. *Skeleton Surfers* is the most northerly roof
crack.

Skeleton Surfers XS 6a **S0** 20 feet (7)
Follow the roof/shelf crack skirting the wall above *Previous Tope-Rope Problem*
until an undercutting move brings you to the rock bridge.
FSA Mike Robertson (3.9.95)

Killer Loop XS 6a **S1** 20 feet (8)
Follow the roof/shelf crack in the opposite direction (spotter advisable for the first
10 feet) until it finishes. A span backwards is required to reach an adjacent crack
which leads to the rock bridge.
FSA Jonathan Cook (3.9.95)

From the ledge above Octopus Weed Cave, a look southwards reveals a yellow-and-
black-streaked arête and groove 80 yards away. The black groove is:

This Is the Life E2 5c **S3** 30 feet (9)
With the necessary high tide, this groove is best attacked from the left. Once
established in the groove, allow yourself a rest before crimping your way to the
final (and hard 5c) move. You will touch down if you don't make it. Superb rock
and some excellent moves.
FSA Pete Oxley (11.5.89)

One Cool Vibe E1 5c **S2** 30 feet (10)
Climb the escapable rounded arête to the left of *This Is the Life*.
FSA Pete Oxley (11.5.89)

Two hundred yards south of the two jib cranes is a waterfall splashing gently into the
sea. Ten yards before (north of) this is a large ledge that can be stepped down to in
order to view the cave which undercuts the entire path by 60 feet!

TOPO B

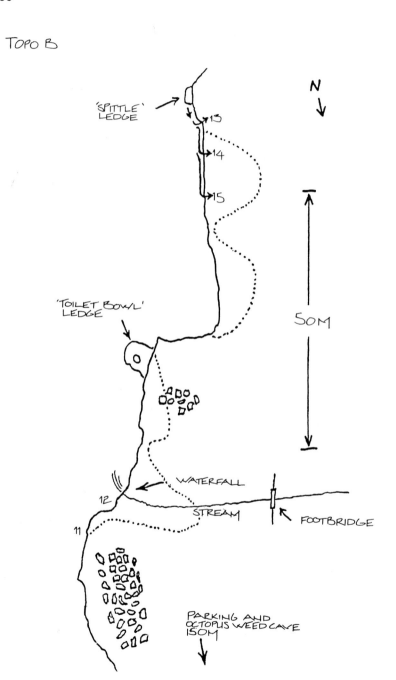

N

'SPITTLE'
LEDGE

13

14

15

'TOILET BOWL'
LEDGE

50M

WATERFALL

12

STREAM

FOOTBRIDGE

11

PARKING AND
OCTOPUS WEED CAVE
150M

The end of this ledge is the top of a bolted route:

Law of the Jungle E5 6b (7b) **S0** 30 feet (11)
This climbs the steep wall from sea-level at the northern end of the entrance to the
cave, across some very steep ground, to the cliff-top path. It has excellent water
below. [NYS]

The top of *Law of the Jungle* is also the start of an excellent (but bolted) very-deep
water solo. This is:

Swinging Nineties E5 6b (7b) **S1** 30 feet (12)
[Frontispiece photo] Step down and crank leftwards into the depths of the cave
along a pocketed break-line. Pause for breath at a poor undercut, and then use it
to lunge horizontally for some poor holds. If you can hang these, you've done the
first half of the crux. Now get fully established on these (...the second half...) and
continue on positive holds to a rock-over finale. Excellent water. Consider allowing
yourself one on-sight solo attempt if you dare. A committing solo owing to the
inverted nature of the crux moves.
FSA Mike Robertson (12.8.95)

North again, 25 yards south of the waterfall, is a large pile of blocks. South of here
the path swings rightwards; at this point three separate caves can be viewed (although
not in their entirety). The long, streaked, east-facing wall encompassing the first two
caves has a number of routes on it. A walk 50 yards south from the large blocks to
the dwindling southern end of the obvious ledge/platform, finds a solitary resin bolt,
about 2 feet from the edge.

Down-climb here (VS) or swing down a short rope – safer, there's a ledge below.
From this ledge swing rightwards (north) to a groove. This is:

Robertson's Jam Very Severe 5a **S1** 20 feet (13)
Testament to the 'crimp-seeking' fingers of 'Tubbs' Taylor. Harder if you don't find
them!
FSA Steve Taylor (13.6.93)

Alternatively, step across the groove and commence battle with:

Spittle 'n' Spume E1 5b/c **S0/1** 25 feet (14)
[Photo p.80c] This swings rightwards and traverses the lip of the cave on good
edges, poor footholds. Terrific climbing. After 15 feet, climb direct to the top.
FSA Mike Robertson (13.6.93)

If you're feeling particularly strong and/or pining for a splashdown situation, how
about:

Bare Reputation XS 6b **S0/1** 45 feet (15)
[Photo p.80c] This follows the *Spittle 'n' Spume* traverse and continues ever
rightwards on less than satisfactory holds. Pumpy and sustained on perfect rock.
You head initially for a large, domed hold sticking out slightly; once you've hung

TOPO C

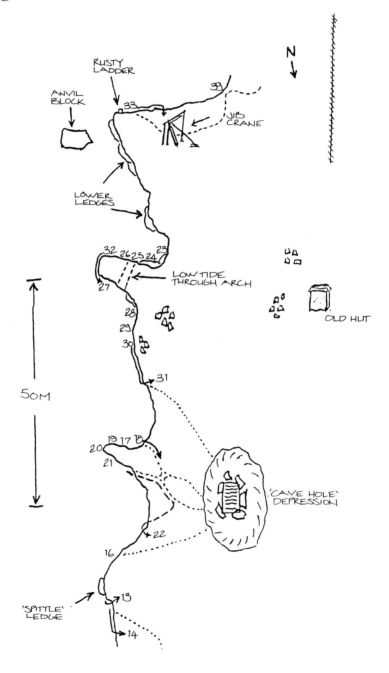

this you've done the crux. Before congratulating yourself, drop down slightly and continue rightwards until jugs show you the way to the top. Approximately F7a+ value, but without the steel. Mike's little test-piece has seen some splashdowns!
FSA Mike Robertson (15.5.95)

From same lower ledge, one last route can be found.

Intimate Dancing Very Severe 5a **S2** 25 feet (16)
This is just south of the other three. It follows the leftward-trending arête on good holds. Technical. Watch the water depth!
FSA Mike Robertson (13.6.93)

Ten yards south of the access bolt (by *Robertson's Jam*) the ledge runs out. Below your feet is a huge cave guarded on its southern periphery by a hanging arête. Under your feet is *Crab Party* and the arête is known as Grotto Arête.

Grotto Arête Sector
Step up to the vegetated rocks and walk south 10 yards to the arête. A large boulder here has a resin abseil bolt on it. This provides access to a ledge at the base of the south-facing wall on the northern extremity of yet another huge cave! A thick, knotted access rope is also in position, at time of writing, allowing entry up and down, without the need for a harness. This access rope will probably be seasonal. Once down to the lower ledge, the first route to be found is:

Captain Haddock XS 5b **S1** 25 feet (17)
This crosses the bottom of the access rope and climbs the wall and capping roof to its right.
FSA Mike Robertson (19.5.95)

Gourmet Shit Traverse XS 5c **S0/1** 40 feet (18)
From the base of Captain Haddock, traverse the entire arête clockwise. How is this possible? Well, after an overhanging section in the depths of the cave, a window shows the way. Crawl through it and continue back round to the starting-point.
FSA Mike Robertson (26.8.95)

Next on the list, right again, is:

Flipper Force XS 6a **S0** 25 feet (19)
Start below the arête, swing up and left, crank onto the face just left of the arête, and follow the face (reachy and technical) to the top. Nice, thin moves.
FSA Damian Cook (19.5.95)

Jonathan Cook was heard to shout, 'Take, take!' as he fell off after snapping a handhold at the top of this one – something which still causes him embarrassment today.

Moving rightwards, standing under the arête you can view a huge niche from below. This is topped by an 8-foot ceiling! Unbelievably, only 5c. This is:

Up the Grotto   XS 5c   **S0/1**   25 feet   (20)
Climb up into the niche. Once fully entombed, climb the ceiling direct on huge flake holds; then swing powerfully around to the right, and exit on the right edge of the arête. Surreal!
FSA Mike Robertson (19.5.95)

Next is:

Ooh, Lovely!   XS 5c   **S0**   25 feet   (21)
This climbs the face on the right of the arête. Climb initially rightwards and swing gradually leftwards to finish on same holds as *Up the Grotto*. Sustained and powerful.
FSA Mike Robertson (19.5.95)

The last route here is found in the cave just north of Grotto Arête. This is:

Crab Party   XS 6a   **S1/2**   70 feet   (22)
Who once said 'Word is that it's all a bit vertical'? Sorry Nic, but you obviously haven't done this one.
Traverse northwards into the cave at 4c/5a, (check the potential above your head), until directly below a huge roof with a line of large, horizontal flake holds and jugs. You can't miss the line (or escape it!). Climb the wall and then the 25-foot roof to a small niche below the lip. Scrunge into this and reach for good holds; continue to top.
A complete adventure in its own right. Brilliant and unmissable. Pumpy, with splashdown potential for E5 leaders? (Sorry, Ian P.) Check water depth carefully!
FSA Mike Robertson (19.5.95)

When standing on top of the Grotto Arête looking south, you can see a leaning, streaked face just past the obvious cave. The face is terminated by an arête. There are a number of routes here. To find these, walk south past the face and the arête to where another bay can be found, marked by a very obvious anvil-shaped block in the sea which is immediately east of another old jib crane. This bay contains yet more routes. These and the streaked face routes are in The Big Easy Sector.

The Big Easy Sector
Note: an obvious water-level indicator exists here: if you can see the 'through-arch' (marked on overhead topo), then it's a little shallow; when the arch is 'filled' go for it! Access is an easy scramble onto a protruding, low ledge 20 yards north of the 'anvil' block.

This is followed by a traverse northward for 20 feet to yet another wide ledge.

Babes and Bedsheets   XS 6a   **S3**   25 feet   (23)
This is the first route. Damp and scary. V-groove, left under large roof, exit. A

Mark Williams (R) and Guy Dixon on
The Laws Traverse Photo: Jonathan Cook

Joff Cook on Animal Magnetism
Photo: Damian Cook

PORTLAND
THE BIG EASY WALL

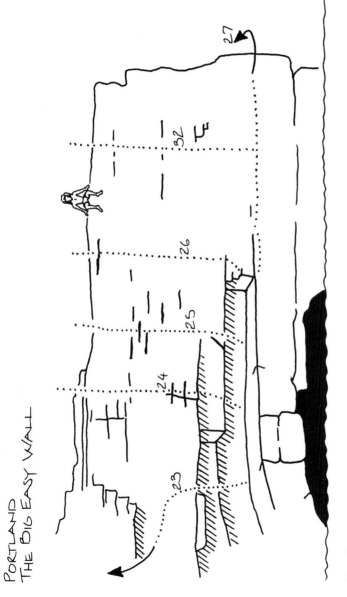

23 BABES AND BEDSHEETS
24 FOXY CHICKS
25 REEL 'EM IN
26 AQUAMARINA
27 THE BIG EASY
32 THE LITTLE HARD

'fall-backwards head-first' crux!
FSA Mike Robertson (6.8.94)

Rather better is:

Foxy Chicks   XS 5c   **S0**   20 feet   (24)
This starts from the middle of the ledge; reach for a huge side-pull (or poor hand-jam); crank! Continue up slots to top.
FSA Mike Robertson (6.8.94)

Even better is:

Reel 'Em In   XS 6a   **S0**   20 feet   (25)
[Photo p.80b] Eight feet right of *Foxy Chicks*. Drop down onto the roof-capped ledge further right. Make a long, blind reach around roof to a generous diagonal hold (a hold-spotter handy!), share on this, and either heel hook or plyometricate yourself up the slotted face! Fun.
FSA Damian Cook (21.5.95)

Aquamarina   XS 6a/b   **S1**   25 feet   (26)
[Photo p.80d] A fingery boulder-problem up the wall right of *Foxy Chicks*. Step right out of the cave under *Foxy Chicks*. Reach up to a horizontal spike and then climb the wall above more or less direct to the top. Scene of five splashdowns before success. Check out your landing-site, and wait for high tide.
FSA Steve Taylor (11.8.95)

Now for the traverse...

The Big Easy   XS 5c   **S0**   60 feet   (27)
From the right-hand end of the roof-capped ledge, traverse rightwards across the technical face to the arête. Continue around the arête (rest); then embark on the other side – overhanging, juggy, and fun (watch out for the odd boulder). When you can sit down you've done it!
FSA Mike Robertson (6.8.94)

To get out without a swim either:
    a. Reverse all of it or
    b. Reverse half of it and escape up the arête at about VS or
    c. Do one of these:

Ixtlan   XS 5b   **S1**   30 feet   (28)
From the large sit-down finishing-ledge of *The Big Easy*, traverse easily rightwards for 25 feet. You should now be below a vague corner/groove topped by a capping roof with much flowstone in its mid-upper section. Go for it. It has a memorable mantel finish, which is probably the crux. This is where your supposed friends will either refuse to help, or tread indifferently on your fingers. Be prepared.
FSA Damian Cook (23.4.95)

If you're feeling stronger (or you've already bagged *Ixtlan*), try:

Karma   XS 5c   **S2**   30 feet   (29)
This is found 10 feet right of *Ixtlan*. Climb the wall on good holds to a domed roof with a flowstone crack running through it (daylight showing through). Climb the roof to a flake and make a hard rock-over move to finish. Sustained, and a little scary.
FSA Mike Robertson (8.5.95)

Feeling cranky? Then do:

Mad about You   XS 5c/6a   **S2**   30 feet   (30)
This route has the slight advantage of a half-height crux. Keep an eye on the boulders. Climb the grey-and-yellow-streaked groove 10-12 feet right of *Karma* until it feels desperate. That means you're on-line. Crank on a small square edge to gain a good jug. Continue on steep rock (sustained) to the top. Swing left, to finish left of the capping roof.
FSA Mike Robertson (15.5.95)

If you enjoyed *Mad about You*, get yourself back down on the *Ixtlan* wall for this little adventure:

Russian Roulette   XS 6a   **S1**   70 feet   (31)
Not as dangerous as the name suggests! More of a gamble as to when you'll fall off... An epic. The first breach of the entire *Ixtlan* wall.
Start on *The Big Easy*, traverse rightwards past *Ixtlan*, *Karma*, and *Mad about You*, and continue for a further 20 feet, to within 5 feet of the diagonal arête on the edge of the cave. You'll be knackered. Now enter the flowstone crack with commitment (crux), and climb rapidly to better holds. At the break, swing left a few feet and finish direct over the juggy roof section. If climbed from *The Big Easy* right through, a total of 130 feet of climbing! Low swell desirable.
FSA Mike Robertson (11.6.95)

Last one here is one you missed on the way around ...

The Little Hard   XS 5c   **S2**   30 feet   (32)
This traverses rightwards across crux of *The Big Easy*; instead of continuing to the arête, climb the groove 6 feet left of the arête direct. Technical. Don't fall from the top move!
FSA Mike Robertson (15.5.95)

There is one more route to bag in the The Big Easy Sector. This is the best introduction to deep water soloing on Portland for five reasons: easy access, it's only HS 4b, the crux is low, it's escapable, and the water is always deep. An all-tide route! A failure means a climb up the old ladder conveniently situated below the old crane, beneath the large, lower ledge, right opposite the 'anvil' block. It is:

Temporary Lifestyle   Hard Severe 4b   **S0**   35 feet   (33)
[Photo p.96a] Down-climb the ladder. Traverse leftwards on the obvious, good break-line. A tricky move up gains a groove (escape possible); then traverse leftwards for 15 feet beneath the capping roofs and top out on jugs, below the old chain.
FSA Mike Robertson (31.7.94)

Desperado Cave
From the crane at the top of *Temporary Lifestyle*, a glance south shows a gigantic cave split by three obvious arêtes. The hideously overhanging southernmost arête is the line of *Lick of the Cat*, and *Desperado* is the route starting from the access ledge at the southern end of the cave, traversing in and wandering diagonally ever upwards. The northernmost, square-cut arête is the swim-in *Surface Tension*, and left of that is the arête of *Pirates of the Black Atlantic*. The finishes are a good deal better than they look!

Starting at the southern end...

Psycho Man   XS 5b   **S1/2**   35 feet   (34)
[Photo p.96a] An entertaining solo through intimidating roofs, with reasonable water. Traverse rightwards on *Desperado* to the start of its crux traverse; then climb directly up on jugs to the roof section. Make a reach up to a huge conglomerate jug (solid, honest!), swing out on this to big slopy finishing holds in a lichenous V-groove in the roof, and a crux mantel. All good fun. Please note that there is a nasty little pointed boulder below the crux. Not a problem at high tide, but if you fall off at anything less than high tide, make sure you do it sideways.
FSA Mike Robertson (10.6.95)

Mike's Free Willy   XS 6a   **S0/1**   35 feet   (35)
A peculiarly named eliminate, starting on the initial traverse of *Desperado* and taking the harder line left of the *Desperado* finish. A cranky and committing roof finish.
FSA Damian Cook (23.7.95)

Desperado   XS 6a   **S0**   60 feet   (36)
An exciting introduction to long 'cavy' routes, with a fierce traverse just above the sea to start. Down-climb from the promontory marked on the topo. Traverse northwards into cave, traverse the pocketed break-line low down with a little difficulty, continue to jugs. Continue diagonally rightwards past an old rusty peg (any info on this ?), up to a large break-line; then trend rightwards to top out on rock which is significantly better than it looks! Atmospheric.
FSA Mike Robertson (9.6.95)

Pirates of the Black Atlantic   XS 5a/b   **S2**   30 feet   (37)
Originally the downclimb for *Lick of the Cat*! Boscombe boy does it again. The middle of the three arêtes. The base of this has a useful ledge to sit on or abseil

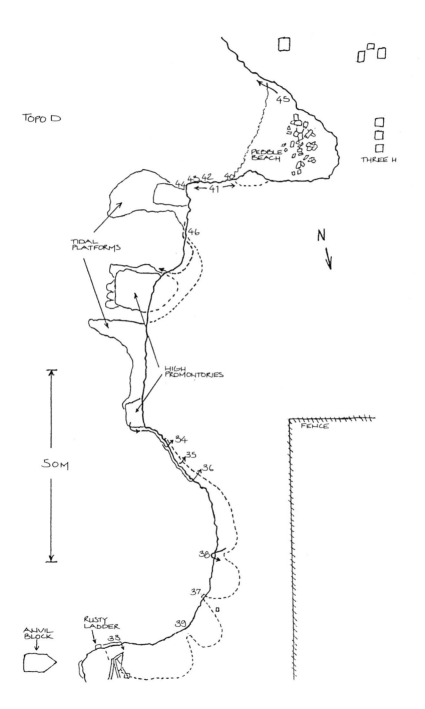

TOPO D

45

PEBBLE
BEACH

THREE H

44 43 42 40
← 41 →

46

N
↓

TIDAL
PLATFORMS

HIGH
PROMONTORIES

FENCE

50M

34

35

36

38

37

ANVIL
BLOCK

RUSTY
LADDER

39

39

down onto. Don't fall onto it though... A mellow route with good holds all the
way. For abseilers, tie to the 'P'-embossed square limestone block next to the path.
FSA Damian Cook (9.6.95)

Lick of the Cat   XS 5c   **S1/2**   35 feet   (38)
The obvious overhanging 45-degree arête. Approach down *Pirates of the Black
Atlantic*. From the bottom ledge, traverse south at 5a until you reach the base of
the arête. Swing underneath it. The route climbs the left-hand/south face of it, so is
less formidable than it looks. But it's pumpy! A superb line, and littered with
excellent holds. A must-do.
FSA Damian Cook (9.6.95)

Surface Tension   XS 5c   **S0/1**   35 feet   (39)
The northernmost square-cut arête in the Desperado Cave. A grossly overhanging
upper section... Good water. The base is inaccessible by normal means. Got a
boat? Alternatively, do as the first ascensionist did; swim across in your grundies
and do it bootless and chalkless! A daring and committing finish, direct over the
roof right (north) of the obvious V-groove.
FSA Mike Robertson (4.8.95)

Too Funky Beach Area
Also known as First Beach, this is located below the first group of three huts found
when walking south. A colourful swimming spot, home of two bolt routes. The left
hand one is:

Too Funky (for Me)   E3 6a   (6c)   **S3**   25 feet   (40)
[Photo p.80a] Traverse in leftwards from the promontary/*Makin' Bacon* arête.
When you reach the second line of bolts, climb up through the roofs to a crux
which is best tackled with a crafty toe-hook. Continue on slots to the top. At very
high tide, the water is only a few feet deep beneath you. Be warned.
FSA Mike Robertson (11.8.95)

More sensibly:

Penny Lane   XS 5b   **S1**   35 feet   (41)
...is the bouldering traverse starting in the back left corner of the beach (as you
walk down to it). Finishes on the promontory. Not entirely a deep water solo, but
an excellent traverse. Reverse it for best value.
FSA Mark Williams (6.8.94)

Starting from *Penny Lane* (from either end), three routes are found. The right-hand
bolt line was on-sight soloed, but then accidentally bolted by a visitor two weeks later.
This is:

Marine Boy   XS 5c   **S1**   25 feet   (42)
From the *Penny Lane* traverse, make some rather blind moves on good holds to
negotiate the left-hand side of the capping roof. Crank and make a long reach for

71

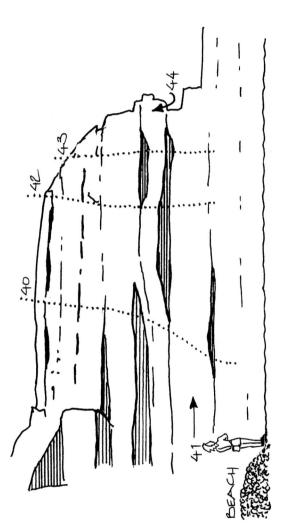

PORTLAND
THE TOO FUNKY WALL

40 TOO FUNKY
41 PENNY LANE
42 MARINE BOY
43 GODZUKI
44 MAKIN' BACON

BEACH

the break – it's done. Biceps useful.
FSA Mike Robertson (10.6.95)

Godzuki XS 5c **S0/S1** 20 feet (43)
Start from the promontory. Swing leftwards around the arête; then climb the
pockets immediately left of the arête. Another one for the biceps.
FSA Damian Cook (9.6.95)

Makin' Bacon XS 5c **S0** 20 feet (44)
The short and playful arête immediately right of *Godzuki*, taken direct. Nearest
thing to gritstone around here.
FSA Mike Robertson (5.8.95)

Memory Lane XS 4c, 5b **S0** 75 feet, 40 feet (45)
A lovely outing, but do it with a good high spring-tide only for best effect. This is
not a safety problem, more an enjoyment consideration. Lower tides detract from
the route's quality and bring the grade down to overall 4c. Good footholds down
there in the water y'see!
FSA Mark Williams, Mike Robertson (6.8.94)

From the Too Funky Beach, looking out to sea, there is a cave about 30 yards to the
left. It can be reached either from the end of the *Penny Lane* traverse or, better, by
dropping in from the cliff-top ledge, down an easy corner. The lip of this cave has
been breached by the following route:

Trashy's Traverse XS 5c **S3** 35 feet (46)
A long, involved traverse, requiring a high level of commitment to hang the
numerous huge hollow flakes. From the lower ledge at the south-west side of the
cave, climb up high to start (large triangular flake); then drop down slightly and
continue the traverse leftwards across the lip of the entire cave. At least one
hands-off rest if you can find it. Huge tide is essential, a 2.4m tide gives about 3½
feet of water. The first ascensionist waited two months for the best conditions.
FSA Mike Robertson (11.8.95)

Lime Kiln Cave Area

A lovely area catching the morning sun. Calm seas are useful, especially on *The
Bellybutton Traverse*. All routes climb flowstone walls and are bolted, if pre-inspection
is the order of the day.

Approach
There are various approaches. The easiest, with respect to parking, is to leave your
car as for the Cave Hole approach.

From the twin cranes, walk north along the shoreline for 500 yards, whereupon a
huge conical mountain-biking 'mound' cannot be missed. Pass this (over the top –

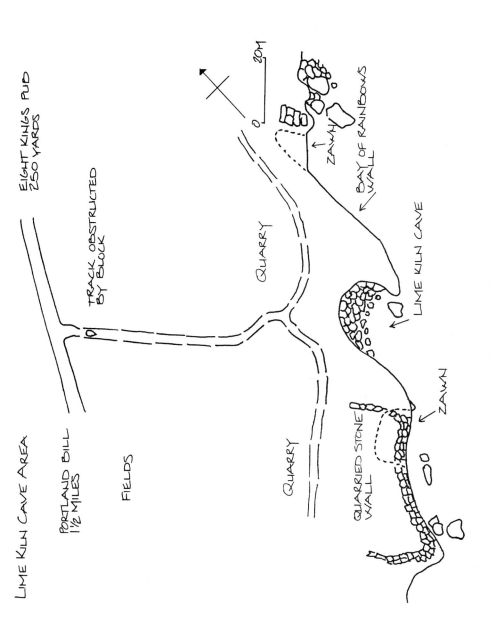

LIME KILN CAVE AREA

PORTLAND BILL
1½ MILES

FIELDS

EIGHT KINGS PUB
250 YARDS

TRACK OBSTRUCTED
BY BLOCK

QUARRY

QUARRY

0

20M

ZAWN

BAY OF RAINBOWS
WALL

LIME KILN CAVE

ZAWN

QUARRIED STONE
WALL

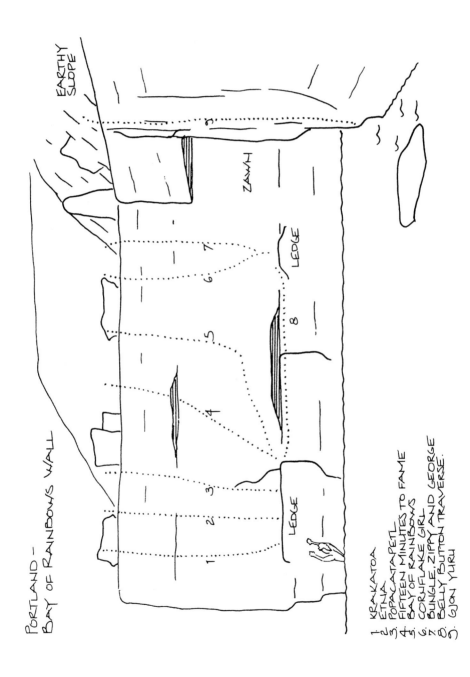

PORTLAND –
BAY OF RAINBOWS WALL

EARTHY SLOPE

ZAWN

LEDGE

LEDGE

LEDGE

1. KRAKATOA
2. ETNA
3. POPACATAPETL
4. FIFTEEN MINUTES TO FAME
5. BAY OF RAINBOWS
6. CORNFLAKE GIRL
7. BUNGLE, ZIPPY AND GEORGE
8. BELLY BUTTON TRAVERSE.
9. GJON YURU

no cheating), continue past some large blocks on the right, and then head gradually rightwards down a scree slope immediately north of a large bowl/amphitheatre.; this is Lime Kiln Cave, also known as The Amphitheatre. Don't walk into this (you'll break a leg), but keep to the left, and scramble over some large boulders to the top of a flowstone-coated wall.

An abseil, from numerous bolts, or a downclimb gives access to most of the routes. The routes are described from left to right, when viewed from their starts on a spacious ledge.

The face has two ledges at its base. There are plentiful belay bolts for abseiling and setting up photo shoots. The first six routes are described from the left-hand ledge.

Etna   Very Severe 4b   **S1**   25 feet
Climb slightly leftward from the left-hand side of the ledge, past some spiky jugs. Watch out for the ledge if you fall.
FSA Steve Taylor (3.4.94)

Popacatapetl   Hard Severe 4a   **S1/S2**   25 feet
The easy, juggy line from the centre of the ledge. Pass some excellent jugs in the flowstone.
FSA Damian Cook (10.4.94)

Krakatoa   E1 5c   (6a)   **S1/S2**   25 feet
Climb the face 6 feet left of the right-hand end of the ledge. A reachy finish awaits! You were warned...
FSA Mike Robertson (27.4.94)

Fifteen Minutes to Fame   E1 5b   (6a)   **S1**   25 feet
More flowstone! Nice climbing, crux finish again. Shares initial starting-holds with *Bay of Rainbows*. The first ascensionist bolted the line, then soloed the first ascent.
FSA Steve Taylor (5.8.94)

Bay of Rainbows   E3 6a   (6c)   **S1**   30 feet
Step off the right-hand end of the lower ledge, continue diagonally rightwards. Excellent moves, with a mid-height crux. A superb and 'innovative' outing.
FSA Damian Cook (16.7.94)

The Bellybutton Traverse   E2 5b   (6a+)   **S0**   35 feet
[Photo p.64b] The superb, rightwards traverse, low down, with enough water at any tide. Jugs all the way. Watch the 'crotch-wetting' blowhole!
FSA Mike Robertson (3.6.94).

For best effect - do it stark naked! To continue, either reverse it or try:

Cornflake Girl   E2 5b   (6a+)   **S1**   25 feet
The best continuation of *The Bellybutton Traverse*. Quite sustained, no real crux. Lots of moulded-in flowstone 'corn flakes'. From the belay on the right-hand side of *The Bellybutton Traverse*, trend diagonally leftwards on the delightful breakfast cereal.
FSA Mike Robertson (3.6.94)

And lastly on this wall:

Bungle, Zippy and George   Very Severe 4c   **S2**   25 feet
The direct line from right-hand end of *The Bellybutton Traverse*. Climb up
flowstone and then through the roof – a mantel finish. Jump off, but don't fall off:
the ledge-system awaits!
FSA Mike Robertson (21.8.94)

Gyonyuru   E3 5c   **S2/3**   30 feet
To the right of the *Bay of Rainbows* wall is a cave. This route climbs the arête on
the right of the cave, up a very steep crack. Scramble up the earthy slope to finish.
FSA Damian Cook (8.95)

The following three solos are on the east-facing wall leading up to the southern
entrance to Lime Kiln Cave itself. They are all reached by abseil from blocks and belay
bolts along the top of the cliff. Take care to avoid disturbing the Portland Sea Lavender
growing on the earthy slopes surrounding Lime Kiln Cave.

Lime Kiln Cave

These routes require a great deal of tenacity and cunning, coupled with the ability to
swim/boulder-hop as required in order to escape, should it all go sadly wrong. The
nearest easy escape point is a Diff ramp 100 yards to the south. Low swell desirable.

The Great Escape (Second Pitch)   E3 5c(6c)   **S2**   55feet
Plenty of commitment (and good water) required for this adventure. Abseil from
blocks to the two-bolt belay (on the southern arête on the entrance to Lime Kiln
Cave) which divides the two pitches of *The Great Escape*. The bench seat
arrangement is most desirable.
Climb leftwards and down slightly on excellent pockets and edges. On reaching
an obvious, good foot-ledge, continue around the blunt arête and climb the
headwall above (much deeper water at this point) on small holds. Continue past
the two-bolt belay in the blocks to the top. [NYS]

Esmerelda's Monkey (Second Pitch)   E5 6b   (7b)   **S2**   65 feet
A true nutter's proposition! This pitch starts as for *The Great Escape*'s second pitch,
but instead of cruising up the headwall, continues traversing leftward into the
bowels of a huge cave, and a three-bolt belay. Very sustained. Top out on jugs to
reach some large quarried blocks. You will need to be very fit to on-sight this one.
At the time of writing, this pitch has yet to be climbed free (roped or otherwise),
and the given grade is speculative. Exceptionally pumpy. [NYS]

Esmerelda's Monkey (Third Pitch)   E5 6a   (7a+)   **S2**   55 feet
[Photo p.16a] A considerable adventure, and not much easier than the second
pitch. Another bench seat affair. From the belay, launch leftwards and attack the
many flat holds crossing the lip of the cave, pausing for breath at a poor knee-bar

(if it fits). Continue leftwards on worsening holds across an undercut headwall, drop down slightly to a large side-pull and a poor rest; then carry on across the blank-looking face (keeping a watchful eye on the boulder lurking below) to a three-bolt belay. You've bagged it, but it's not quite over:

either fall into the sea;

or use the belay to gain the hidden flake and easy ground to the left;

or, very ethically, ignore the belay bolts, perform one last desperate move to pass them and gain the flake crack, and then follow this to the quarried blocks and an entourage of enthusiastic onlookers.

Allow yourself a pat on the back.

FSA Mike Robertson (20.4.96)

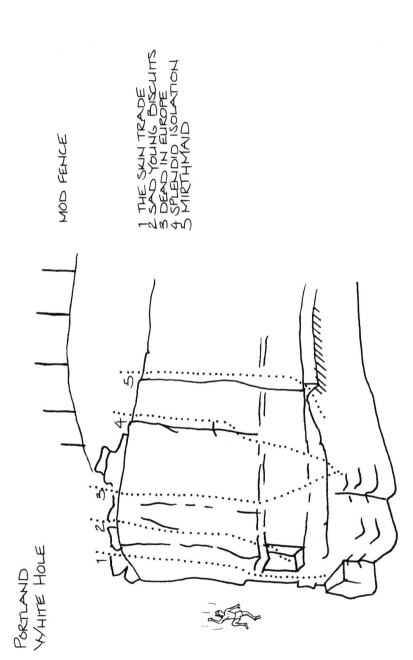

PORTLAND
WHITE HOLE

MOD FENCE

1 THE SKIN TRADE
2 SAD YOUNG BISCUITS
3 DEAD IN EUROPE
4 SPLENDID ISOLATION
5 MIRTHMAD

White Hole

An atmospheric and imposing place to solo! Quite 'bottly', especially when it's choppy, windy, or cold. Wait for the best weather!

Five solos here; but only two have had 'legitimate' ascents.

As in Lime Kiln Cave, all routes are fully bolted.

Approach

From *The Eight Kings Inn* (see Cave Hole Approach), drive southwards down the B3154, past the twin cranes turn-off, and continue all the way to Portland Bill, where there is a large car-park, a stone's throw from a lighthouse. A free parking alternative is available in a lay-by, 400 yards before the car-park, on the right.

From the far side of the car-park, skirt the DRA establishment fence on its left and continue to follow the fence around to the right, keeping it at your elbow. You'll come to the tip of a long, sea-filled gully; scamper past this and then immediately drop down leftwards onto the obvious square promontory with its resident boulders.

All routes, excepting the *Project*, are approached by using abseil bolts among the boulders. *The Skin Trade* starts from a luxurious ledge below the west face, *Sad Young Biscuits* tackles the grooved arête from a handy sentry-box belay, the remaining three routes are ideally tackled using a hanging bench seat (see tactics) from their shared belay in the depths of the gully – the south-east face.

The *Project* is found immediately over the water, in the bolted area of White Hole South. It is the left-hand bolt line as you view the crag from its base, a little left of the disused waste pipe.

The Skin Trade   E4 6a   (6c+)   S2   40 feet
Just left of the south-east arête. To reach this route, abseil from a two-bolt belay down the south face to a good standing-ledge.
Climb rightwards into a hanging niche and negotiate this with difficulty to a crack. Continue rightwards to an obvious ledge on the arête. Reflect a little, and commit to a series of thin and balancy moves up the wall just left of the bolt line; the difficulty eases a little just before the top. Soloed in less than ideal conditions by a very motivated 'Tubbs' Taylor.
FSA Steve Taylor (15.8.94)

Sad Young Biscuits   E4 6b   (7a+)   S2   30 feet
Abseil from bolts down the overhanging groove left (looking out) of the south-east arête. From the belay in the sentry-box, climb rightwards slightly, then direct, up the groove. Continue to the top and a mantel finish. The crux is low down, but it's fingery and intense, and the first (roped) ascensionist can't seem to repeat it. Don't expect a stroll in the park. Reasonable water at high tide. [NYS]

The next three routes share a belay. A bench seat is desirable. They are all very photogenic, so wear your best lycra and boots.

Dead in Europe   E4 6b   (7a+)   **S2**   35 feet
From the belay, climb up and left to good holds. Crank leftwards to an obvious layback rib. Slap and balance up the rib until it finishes. Make a full-on barn-door slap for a crimp. If you can catch it, you've bagged the crux. Continue more easily to the top. Excellent photo opportunities.
FSA Mike Robertson (15.8.94)

Splendid Isolation   E3 6a   (6c)   **S2/S3**   35 feet
The thin flake crack right again. Climb directly up from the belay to the base of the flake crack. Balance your way precariously up this to the last two moves, which are the crux. Check the water carefully, it's a long way down! Please wait for high tide. [NYS]

Mirthmaid   E4 6b   (7a+)   **S2/S3**   35 feet
A low crux makes this fairly amenable, but it's hard! From the belay, climb up and right to the back of the roof. Span across the roof for good holds on the lip. The next couple of moves are very powerful and you don't get long to check them out. Once they are done, however, the rest of the route up the thin crack is easy. [NYS]

Project   E6 6c   (7c+)   **S1**   25 feet
One more potential (bolted) solo is found here, in the southern section of White Hole. It takes the line just left of the waste-pipe shown on the overhead topo. It is presently an F7c+ project; purists would call it XS 6c! [NYS]

Jane Wylie on *Octopus Weed*
Photo: Jonathan Cook

Mike Robertson on *Too Funky (for Me)*
Photo: Helen Heanes

Guy Dixon on *Spittle 'n' Spume*
Photo: Steve Taylor

Damian Cook ...off *Bare Reputation*
Photo: Jonathan Cook

Steve Taylor on *Aquamarina* Photo: Guy Dixon

Tim Dunsby on *Purple Shorts* Photo: Nigel Coe

Dead In Europe

I lay on my belly and peered over the edge. The circling seagulls stepped up the cacophony and edged ever closer, as if willing me to fall off. I paid little attention; I was enraptured. Why does limestone look so inspiring when it's devoid of appreciable holds?

In my mind's eye I was already cranking on the unspoilt tinies, slowly pumping out, increasingly technical moves propelling me ever closer to the top. A slap, a smear of a toe, a lunge, and it's all over. Now back to the real world. Back to the car to extricate the necessary power.

Beginnings of a short yet torrid love affair. I can't explain. If you understand, you do. If you don't, you don't. Shall I continue? The weeks surged on. I flirted briefly with the central groove. I danced and even boogied on the grooved arête. Almost a sad friend. I entertained the idea of the most northerly face; and how I dreamed! My dreams are mine and this one I held close. Later I sat and smiled, and contemplated a victory more precious than gold. Is that so hard to understand? The aches of success, so very sweet.

More time passed, and I returned. Gaps are what friends are made of. I swung, I dallied, and I even laughed a little. Europe looming close now; not much time left for this baby. The time had come to dance again. My feet were hard to find, and those ballroom sequences proved elusive; yet I persisted and won.

So, here again. The sea invites me today, in its own sweet language. I look up. Sequences remembered? The waves ebb and flow, beckon and intimidate. Deep? I think so. But too late now. I feel free, ropeless, without encumbrances. The ultimate tango. My fingers lead me up to the first break. 5c here, no problems, relax, shake. Step left, shake again. The adrenal rush begins. Share, left again, up a little, smear with the right, heel-hook with the left. The moment of truth. Move up, slap, up again, yet another slap. Still in the running. Crux now, keep it together... rock up, lock it, look where you're going, there it is, that far away?. No time, do it... I catch the sloper, hold it, just, lock it, slap again for the jug.

And so it was, excitement over, the disappointment of the ocean revealed in the gleam of its swell. Time to depart. Until the next time. I think it must be love.

Development of White Hole North, Portland,
and return in late summer to solo
Dead in Europe E4 6b (7a+)

Mike Robertson
(new router, deep water soloer, nutter)

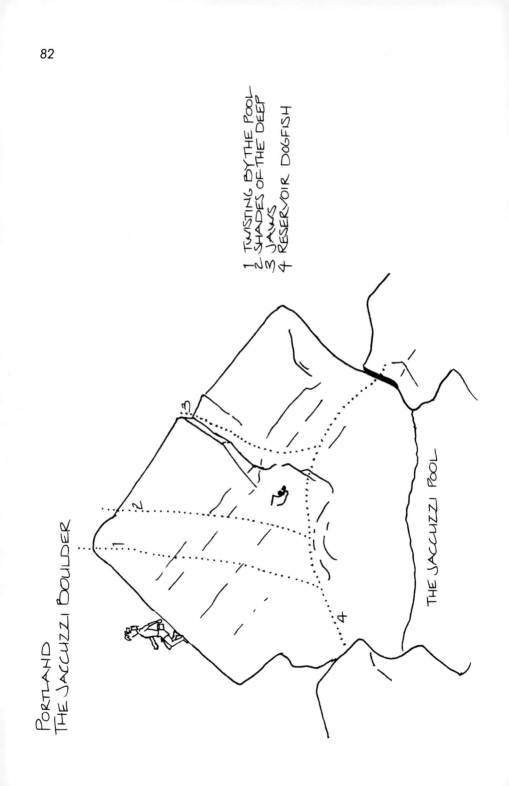

PORTLAND
THE JACCUZZI BOULDER

1 TWISTING BY THE POOL
2 SHADES OF THE DEEP
3 JAWS
4 RESERVOIR DOGFISH

THE JACCUZZI POOL

Jacuzzi Boulder

Located 25 yards north of 'The Triple Boulders', below Blacknor South. Approach via a track below *The Last Rose of Summer* at Blacknor South 9see Portland map p.54). Four excellent boulder-problem routes on a very steep pocketed slab with a rather convenient pool residing below it. Swell/high tide presents problems. A good venue low/mid tide. West-facing, best ticked from early afternoon onwards. Fantastic swimming and diving.

Approach

Drive southwards into Weston, turn right into Westcliffe Road (opposite the shops), follow it to the two phone boxes at the T-junction, turn left into Grangecroft Road, and continue to the car-park. A 200-yard walk to the cliff-top reveals Sharbutts Quarry. A scramble through the trenches of the quarry (heading leftwards) gives access to the huge bolted cliffs of Blacknor South. Once at the base of the cliff, follow the obvious path right (north) along the crag's base until, after about 100 yards, a cave entrance can be seen, about 20 feet up the face. At this point (under *The Last Rose of Summer*, for those familiar with the crag) a tiny, meandering path leads down the scree, in roughly a north-westerly direction. Follow this all the way down towards the sea, and continue boulder-hopping northwards through an assortment of large boulders, until the Jacuzzi Boulder is reached, its steep west face lavishly based with a fine and relatively deep rock-pool.

Twisting by the Pool   XS   5c   **S1**   25 feet
[Photo p.96b] Bottom left, towards the centre; then trend slightly leftwards towards the top. Don't hit the boulder you've just stepped off!!
FSA Mike Robertson (8.5.95)

Shades of the Deep   XS   5c   **S0**   20 feet
Traverse the first 6 feet of the previous route; then follow the pockets diagonally rightwards all the way to the top. The best line on the face. Name? There's a pair of sunglasses in there somewhere!
FSA Mike Robertson (1.5.95)

Jaws   XS   5c   **S0**   20 feet
The arête/groove on the right. Can be done using a number of methods.
FSA Mike Robertson (8.5.95)

Reservoir Dogfish   XS   5b   **S0**   15 feet
The obvious low traverse. A gladiator-style battle for the first ascent!
FSA Damian Cook (8.5.95)

There are two other isolated routes in the vicinity of the Jacuzzi Boulder. Ten yards to the south is found a north-facing boulder with a useful pool at its base. On this is:

Limpet-Fest   XS   5b   **S0**   20 feet
The traverse. Drop down to the water-line from the left and traverse rightwards,

tapping on the limpets prior to crimping them. This is to make them clamp to the rock surface to repel outside attack. It has the added advantage of making them suitable for cranking on!
FSA Jonathan Cook (8.7.95)

The last route in the area is on The Triple Boulders, a group of large boulders about 50 yards south of the Jacuzzi Boulder. One boulder has two bolted lines on its slab and is undercut by water on its right-hand side.

The Last Suitcase before the Holocaust E1 5b **S1** 20 feet
Start in the centre of the slab, beneath the right-hand bolt line. Climb diagonally rightwards above the deep pool to finish.
FSA Steve Taylor (28.8.93)

and to finish:

Night Glue E5 6b (7a+) **S3** 70 feet
OK, so it's not on the south coast. Who cares? Lower Pen Trwyn, we're on your case. Abseil to the high-water-mark at a good high tide with your bench seat, using the bolt runners to maintain contact with the rock. Jettison your harness and make a balancy move to gain the slab. Climb up through the steep section, trending rightwards to a large jug/ledge. Make some thin moves, with a large reach to a good hold and continue more easily to the top. After congratulating yourself, abseil back in to retrieve your bench seat and contemplate your (in)sanity. Anyone selling a boat?

Jumps and Assorted Silliness:

Jumps are always good fun, and essential practice for those shallow ticks. Remember tides and always go in and check the depth if unsure. The highest jump is the arête of *The Skin Trade*, at around 35 to 40 feet.

For the easy and accessible, try these:
Off the ledge above *Temporary Lifestyle*, by the single crane, various heights possible.
Off the waterfall ledge, above *The Swinging Nineties*. Good water.
Off the ledge above *Octopus Weed*, by the twin cranes, risky at low tide.

For the slightly madder:
Run flat out off the grass above *Surface Tension*, into the northern end of the Desperado Cave.
Hurl yourself off the top of *Bay of Rainbows* at Lime Kiln Cave.
Drop tidily off the arête of *The Skin Trade*, White Hole – high and not very deep.

For the insane:
Run extremely fast, and diagonally, off the top of *Marine Boy* at the Too Funky Beach – but do it only at high tide – its a mere 3-5 feet deep, and you will touch the bottom.

More Pleasure:
Highly recommended is the sea-level traverse, at low tide, from *Octopus Weed*, through to *Crab Party*. No climbing or swimming necessary. Fantastic rock architecture, with some amazing colours. Safe even with a little swell. Old trainers recommended.

First Solo Ascents

Please refer to page 22 for an explanation of the first solo ascent styles.

	The Subnutcracker Traverse Unknown
	Paradise Street Unknown
	Helix Unknown
	Freeborn Man probably Nick Buckley [Style 5]
	Halcyon Days Unknown
	The Great Shark Hunt Pete Oxley [Style 1]
	A Bridge Too Far Unknown
1983 June 26	**The Conger** Nick Buckley *The subject of the 1986 guide cover shot, the ultimate inspiration.*
1985 July 15	**Troubled Waters** Pete Oxley [Style 1]
1986 Sept 8	**Donald, Where's Your Trousers?** Crispin Waddy [Style 1]
1986 Sept 8	**Fathoms** Crispin Waddy [Style 1]
1988 April 28	**Camel Filter** Jon Williams [Style 1]
1988 June	**The Hump** Jon Williams [Style 1]
1988 Aug 1	**The Musharagi Tree** Jon Biddle/Jon Williams [Style 1]
1988 Aug	**Slap Ya Dromedary** Jon Williams [Style 1]
1988 Aug	**Numb Bum** Jon Williams [Style 1]
1988 Sept 6	**The Anarchy Stampede** Jon Biddle [Style 3]
1989 March	**Furious Pig** Crispin Waddy [Style 1]
1989 May 11	**This Is The Life** Pete Oxley [Style 1]
1989 May 11	**One Cool Vibe** Pete Oxley [Style 1]
1989 July 2	**Sardine Liberation Front** Andy Donson [Style 1]
1989 Aug 24	**Turkish Delight** Andy Donson [Style 1]
1990 May 23	**The Maypole** Jon Williams [Style 1]
1990 May	**Jon Williams Traverse** eponymous [Style 3]
1990 Aug 3	**Jellied** Jon Biddle [Style 3] *First flashed ascent S Taylor.*
1990 Aug 8	**...And Captain Blood's Cavern** Jonathan Cook [Style 1] *The Boscombe Boys appear on the scene. Scene of a mighty lob by Damian Cook.*
1990 Aug	**The Rise and Dear Demise of the Funky Nomadic Tribes** The Cook Brothers [Style 1] *Down-climbed on-sight to do Fathoms.*
1990 Sept 11	**Snap Crackle and Plop** Dominic Cook [Style 3] *Whiplash splashdown before success.*
1991 July 20	**Truth, Justice and the Ragamuffin Way** Jon Biddle [Style 1]
1991 July 21	**Captain Bastard Got There First** Jonathan Cook [Style 1]
1991 July 21	**Last Season's Loozas** The Cook Brothers [Style 1]
1991 July 22	**Herbert the Turbot** Jon Biddle [Style 3] *This route has baffled several would-be second ascensionists.*
1991 July	**Does Leviathan Plop Float?** Damian Cook [Style 1]
1992 May 23	**Sliding down the Banister** Pete Oxley [Style 1]
1993 May 29	**The Laws Traverse** Pete Oxley [Style1] *There was a race for the first ascent, with three others also jockeying for position on the first moves.*
1993 June 4	**Amazonia** Jonathan Cook [Style 1]
1993 June 13	**Robertson's Jam** Steve Taylor [Style 1]
1993 June 13	**Spittle 'n' Spume** Mike Robertson [Style 1] *His first solo new route. Photos of the first ascent have appeared in magazines and guides.*
1993 June 13	**Intimate Dancing** Mike Robertson [Style 1]
1993 June 26	**The Walkin' Dude** Mike Robertson [Style 1] *Soloed in extremely dangerous conditions, the first ascensionist unable to wait for the required spring-tide, made his*

ascent at low tide.

1993 June	**Leap of Faith** Damian Cook [Style 1] *After swimming to the base of the route with boots and chalkbag tied to his head.*
1993 June	**Tsunami** Damian Cook [Style 3]
1993 Aug 28	**The Last Suitcase before the Holocaust** Steve Taylor [Style 1]
1993 Summer	**Horny L'il Devil** Pete Oxley [Style 5]
1993 Summer	**Mark of the Beast** Pete Oxley [Style 5] *Unrepeated.*
1993 Summer	**Stagedivin'** Pete Oxley [Style 5] *On-sighted by John Fletcher.*
1994 April 3	**Etna** Steve Taylor [Style 5]
1994 April 10	**Popacatapetl** Damian Cook [Style 2]
1994 April 27	**Krakatoa** Mike Robertson [Style 5]
1994 June 3	**The Bellybutton Traverse** Mike Robertson [Style 5]
1994 June 3	**Cornflake Girl** Mike Robertson [Style 5]
1994 July 16	**Bay of Rainbows** Damian Cook [Style 4] *On-sighted by John Fletcher.*
1994 July 30	**Route 66** Mike Robertson [Style 1]
1994 July 31	**Temporary Lifestyle** Mike Robertson [Style 1]
1994 July	**Animal Magnetism** Jonathan Cook [Style 5] *Just for the photos.*
1994 Aug 5	**Fifteen Minutes to Fame** Steve Taylor [Style 1] *Who bolted the line, then soloed it rather than wait for the glue to dry.*
1994 Aug 6	**Memory Lane** Mark Williams (pitch 1) Mike Robertson (pitch 2) [Style 1]
1994 Aug 6	**Penny Lane** Mark Williams [Style 1]
1994 Aug 6	**Babes and Bedsheets** Mike Robertson [Style 1] *In dangerous conditions, with only 2 feet of water below.*
1994 Aug 6	**Foxy Chicks** Mike Robertson [Style 1]
1994 Aug 6	**The Big Easy** Mike Robertson [Style 1]
1994 Aug 14	**Llama Roundabout** Mike Robertson [Style 1] *A three-man FA, with rear man Mark Arnall splashing heavily.*
1994 Aug 15	**The Skin Trade** Steve Taylor [Style 4] *His first [roped] attempt had seen a fall due to a broken foothold.*
1994 Aug 15	**Dead in Europe** Mike Robertson [Style 5] *The insecure nature of this route entices Robertson into a solo ascent.*
1994 Aug 21	**Bungle, Zippy and George** Mike Robertson [Style 2]
1994 Aug	**Davy Jones' Lock-off** Crispin Waddy [Style 1]
1995 April 23	**Ixtlan** Damian Cook [Style 1]
1995 May 1	**Shades of the Deep** Damian Cook [Style 1]
1995 May 8	**Jaws** Mike Robertson [Style 1]
1995 May 8	**Reservoir Dogfish** Damian Cook [Style 1]
1995 May 8	**Twisting by the Pool** Mike Robertson [Style 1]
1995 May 8	**Purple Shorts** Guy Dixon [Style 1]
1995 May 8	**Octopus Weed** Damian Cook [Style 1]
1995 May 8	**Previous Top-Rope Problem** Damian Cook [Style 1] *The name is a dig at a local guidebook author, who used this phrase to belittle true first ascents.*
1995 May 8	**Karma** Mike Robertson [Style 1]
1995 May 15	**Bare Reputation** Mike Robertson [Style 3] *First tentatively viewed in 1993, but dismissed as 'probably impossible'.*
1995 May 15	**Mad about You** Mike Robertson [Style 1]
1995 May 15	**The Little Hard** Mike Robertson [Style 1]
1995 May 19	**Captain Haddock** Mike Robertson [Style 1]
1995 May 19	**Flipper Force** Damian Cook [Style 1]
1995 May 19	**Up the Grotto** Mike Robertson [Style 1]
1995 May 19	**Ooh, Lovely!** Mike Robertson [Style 1]
1995 May 19	**Crab Party** Mike Robertson [Style 1] *Found whilst fishing out his car keys.*
1995 May 21	**Reel 'Em In** Damian Cook [Style 1]

1995 June 9	**Godzuki** Damian Cook [Style 1]
1995 June 9	**Desperado** Mike Robertson [Style 1]
1995 June 9	**Pirates of the Black Atlantic** Damian Cook [Style 1] *Soloed first as a downclimb.*
1995 June 9	**Lick of the Cat** Damian Cook [Style 1]
1995 June 10	**Psycho Man** Mike Robertson [Style 1]
1995 June 10	**Marine Boy** Mike Robertson [Style 1]
1995 June 11	**Russian Roulette** Mike Robertson [Style 1] *A 30-minute epic.*
1995 July 5	**Laws Direct Start** Mike Robertson [Style 3] *Four knee-deep splashdowns before the appropriate sloper was located.*
1995 July 8	**Limpet-Fest** Jonathan Cook [Style 1]
1995 July 23	**Mike's Free Willy** Damian Cook [Style 1]
1995 July 27	**Tentacle Master** Jonathan Cook [Style 3] *Two dramatic splashdowns before eventual success.*
1995 Aug 1	**Escobar** Jonathan Cook [Style 3] *Two seasons to complete.*
1995 Aug 1	**Contortions** Mike Robertson [Style 1]
1995 Aug 4	**Surface Tension** Mike Robertson [Style 1]
1995 Aug 5	**Makin' Bacon** Mike Robertson [Style 1]
1995 Aug 5	**Showtime** Jonathan Cook [Style 3] *Several splashdowns occurred before Joff managed this one.*
1995 Aug 11	**Aquamarina** Steve Taylor [Style 3] *Five splashdowns before the sequence was sorted.*
1995 Aug 11	**Too Funky (for Me)** Mike Robertson [Style 5] *Feasible only at the highest spring-tide.*
1995 Aug 11	**Trashy's Traverse** Mike Robertson [Style 1] *Soloed on the highest spring-tide of the summer.*
1995 Aug 12	**The Swinging Nineties** Mike Robertson [Style 5] *A previous solo attempt resulted in whiplash after a flake hold snapped off.*
1995 Aug 14	**The Gates of Greyskull** Jonathan Cook [Style 5] *Hard on his heels was Robertson, who was unable to make a roped ascent, but discovered that soloing it gave him the required drive to succeed.*
1995 Aug 16	**The Lip Traverse** Dominic Cook [Style 1]
1995 Aug 22	**Crazy Notion** Mike Robertson [Style 1] *He briefly considered bolting this one, but couldn't wait.*
1995 Aug 26	**Gourmet Shit Traverse** Mike Robertson [Style 1]
1995 Aug	**Lower than Whale Shit** Gideon Fitch/Damian Cook [Style 1]
1995 Aug	**Gyonyuru** Damian Cook [Style 1]
1995 Sept 3	**Skeleton Surfers** Mike Robertson [Style 3] *Success came after splashdown when attempting the line from the far corner of the cave.*
1995 Sept 3	**Killer Loop** Jonathan Cook [Style 1] *Three spotters on the FA.*
1995 Sept 19	**El Guapo** Jonathan Cook [Style 3]
1995 Sept 24	**Here Comes the Hizbollah** Mike Robertson [Style 5]
1995 Sept 24	**Lucretia, My Reflection** Mike Robertson [Style 5]
1995 Sept 29	**The Pump Will Tear Us Apart** Mike Robertson [Style 5] *An excellent effort in eerie conditions.*
1995 Sept	**Magician's Trap** Dominic Cook [Style 3] *Dominic's initial attempts were captured on film for the programme Under the Sky, Above the Sea.*
1995 Oct 7	**FYB** Mike Robertson [Style 2] *Only minutes after the bolted first ascent.*
1995 Summer	**Swordfish Trombones** Andy Donson [Style 1]
1996 April 20	**Esmerelda's Monkey** (pitch 3) Mike Robertson [Style 4] *The first attempt resulted in a dip in 8ºC water, when a foothold snapped.*

The Future – Over to You

And now it's time for you to get in on the act. Should you be the pioneering/nails sort, there's scope in the world of deep water soloing for you to make a name for yourself. You could be the contender Marlon Brando wished he had been.

First, of course, there are the Not Yet Soloed routes. Obviously these routes have NYS beside them because most of them are either deadly (*Mariner's Graveyard*) or desperate (*Adrenachrome*). But out there somewhere there is someone with the talent and the cojones to go for the first on-sight solo of *Adrenachrome*.

Connor Cove has a number of unrealized solos, including approaching the chimney of *The Conger* from the back of The Conger Cave. If someone does it soon we'll have to shelve our plans to bolt plastic jugs all the way back there (only joking). There are at least two direct lines to go from midway along *...And Captain Bloods Cavern*, both bold but with great water.

A mile further west lies Hedbury Cove, and this area has recently shown itself to hold some fine soloable lines. We're just waiting for the summer to hit it.

Over at Stair Hole there are several excellent challenges for those with multiple pairs of boots and/or sponsorship. The inside of the West Cave holds the aforementioned suspected E6 link-up of *Escobar* through to *El Guapo*. Another fine challenge is to start on the hanging slab at the end of *El Guapo* and traverse out to the crux of *Herbert the Turbot*. Is it possible? *The Gates of Greyskull* needs to be finished as for *Animal Magnetism* and vice-versa. All this once the ban is lifted, of course.

As for Portland, there are two major roof lines left of *Crab Party*. There are also two lines above the traverse of *The Big Easy*, before *Ixtlan* – both require huge reaches or a massive amount of strength. Desperado Cave still holds numerous very steep roof challenges.

So far, the attitude to deep water soloing has been a bit provincial, but it seems improbable that Dorset is the only county with cliffs that could support such a scene. Berry Head in Devon has shown some promise, with the long *The Magical Mystery Tour* traverse, but further development is needed. Also what about Pembroke, Cornwall, North Wales?

It seems evident that the future will lead soloists abroad in search of more exotic venues, with hotter summers and warmer, bluer seas under steeper, more pocketed limestone. The Mediterranean seems a logical place to search. The Ionian Islands will inevitably boast such locations. Should you be lucky enough to stumble on such a place, please send photos and we'll be on the next plane out.

Rumours abound locally of deep water soloing catching on in Majorca, with a young Spaniard taking up the initiative. So on future holidays to these resorts you'll be able to pack your old slippers – leave your girlfriend to doss on the beach whilst you head off to crank wildly cool solos. That's not sexist, is it?

Index

Accident Procedure

First Aid
If spinal or head injuries are suspected, do not move the patient without skilled help, except to maintain breathing.

If breathing has stopped, clear the airways and start artificial respiration. Do not stop until expert opinion has diagnosed death.

Stop bleeding by applying direct pressure.

Summon help.

Rescue
In the event of an accident where further assistance is required, **dial 999** and ask for the **Coastguard**. The Coastguards are responsible for the co-ordination of all sea-cliff rescues, and will co-ordinate the other services such as helicopters, lifeboats, cliff rescue teams, etc.

It is important to report the exact location and details of the accident and also to have someone meet the rescue team to guide them to the spot.

Nearest Phone Points
Portland & Lulworth Cove – Both within easy reach of a phone.

Durdle Door – At the top of the hill behind the arch is a phone box by a caravan-park; this is closer than Lulworth Cove itself.

The Durlston Country Park Cliffs – There is a 999-only phone by the entrance to the lighthouse.

Local Hospitals
The walking wounded can receive treatment in the casualty departments of the following hospitals:

Weymouth & District Hospital, Melcombe Avenue, Weymouth.
Phone number (01305) 772211.

Swanage Hospital, Queens Road, Swanage.
Phone number (01929) 422282.

Poole General Hospital, Longfleet Road, Poole.
Phone number (01202) 675100.

Helicopter

In the event of a Helicopter evacuation, **all** climbers on or off the cliff should take heed. A helicopter flying close to the cliff will make verbal communication very difficult and small stones will be dislodged by the rotor downdraught. All loose equipment should be secured and climbers in precarious positions should try to make themselves safe.

The people with the injured person should try to identify their location. **No** attempt should be made to throw a rope at the helicopter, but assistance should be given to the helicopter crew if requested. Do not touch the lowered crew member or his winch wire until the trailing wire has earthed the helicopter's static electricity.

Follow-Up

After an accident, a written report should be sent to the Mountain Rescue Committee Statistics Officer, Mr David Noott, Gorsefield, Springbank, New Mills, Stockport, SK 12 4BH, giving details of: date, extent of injuries, and name, age, and address of the casualty. Normally this will be done by the police or local rescue team involved, who will also require the names and addresses of those climbing with the injured party.

Equipment Failure

If unreasonable equipment failure is suspected, then the British Mountaineering Council's technical committee may wish to investigate; contact the BMC at 177-179 Burton Road, West Didsbury, Manchester, M20 2BB.

A Letter From Budapest

We all have our own favourite places, made special by moods and memories, atmospheres and conditions. A more open mind could point out that we are already deeply conditioned, but if I am colour-blind, I am most fortunate that it is my favourite colour that I can see clearest.

In a land-locked city my eyes are drawn, my attention and imagination captured by a natural uncut boulder nestled unassumingly beside a more widely appreciated tourist spectacle. As if that boulder had burst through the surface of my thoughts, my memory is cast back to that place where the hills meet the sea, where my naked body is submerged in the most vivid blues and greens, greys and silver.

When the orchestra stops, the soloist begins. It's the time to put aside all life, all thoughts but one. The safety net is gone. That celebration of certainty and independence is an enormous gamble. One wrong note, one misplaced finger and the curtain will fall. But the unthinkable happens, the hand fumbles and the price of failure must be paid. Yet then, facing the abyss, the dark veil is lifted. This isn't the abyss. There are the most vivid colours – here are our favourite greens and blues and silver.

Beside the ocean we are never alone. From here all life originates. Here we are protected from the worst excesses of gravity, from the urban development, from taking ourselves too seriously. At our favourite places are our friends, and it is our friends that make life colourful. Even in exile my life is flavoured thus, and as I walk through this land-locked city I can taste the salt spray on my lips, and I can hear the waves in my friends' laughter.

Damian Cook

Budapest, October 1995

Mike Robertson on *Psycho Man*
Photo: Steve Taylor

Carol Robertson on *Temporary lifestyle*
Photo: Steve Taylor

Damian Cook *Twisting by the Pool* Photo: Jonathan Cook